HER COUCH OF SILENCE

*A Collection of Poems and the epic poem,
Her Couch of Silence*

Mitchell A. Kramer

iUniverse, Inc.
Bloomington

Her Couch of Silence
A Collection of Poems and the epic poem, Her Couch of Silence

Copyright © 2012 by Mitchell A. Kramer

All rights reserved. No part of this book may be used or reproduced by any means, graphic, electronic, or mechanical, including photocopying, recording, taping or by any information storage retrieval system without the written permission of the publisher except in the case of brief quotations embodied in critical articles and reviews.

The views expressed in this work are solely those of the author and do not necessarily reflect the views of the publisher, and the publisher hereby disclaims any responsibility for them.

iUniverse books may be ordered through booksellers or by contacting:

iUniverse
1663 Liberty Drive
Bloomington, IN 47403
www.iuniverse.com
1-800-Authors (1-800-288-4677)

Because of the dynamic nature of the Internet, any web addresses or links contained in this book may have changed since publication and may no longer be valid. The views expressed in this work are solely those of the author and do not necessarily reflect the views of the publisher, and the publisher hereby disclaims any responsibility for them.

Any people depicted in stock imagery provided by Thinkstock are models, and such images are being used for illustrative purposes only.

Certain stock imagery © Thinkstock.

ISBN: 978-1-4697-9173-9 (sc)
ISBN: 978-1-4697-9175-3 (hc)
ISBN: 978-1-4697-9174-6 (e)

Printed in the United States of America

iUniverse rev. date: 4/30/2012

PREFACE

    I am grateful for my wonderful family, my wife, Judith, my daughter and law partner, Barbara Kramer, and her husband, Steven Acker, and their children, Alex, Eva, Anna, LeeAnn, Evan and Jared; and my son and daughter-in-law, Mitchell F. and Christine Kramer.

    I want to thank the following people for their invaluable assistance in the completion of this collection. Foremost is my wife, Judith Kramer, who edited and made sense of my unpunctuated poems. My son, Mitchell Kramer, and my friends, Judith Schur and Philip Margolis, who suggested changes and corrections to the title poem. My secretaries, Darlene Lubienski and Maureen Coyle, who devoted substantial time to type and format this collection.

    I must also acknowledge my Dartmouth Philosophy Professor Eugene Rosenstock-Huessy who inspired the framework of the title poem and the woman of the couch, whose name I have never known.

Mitchell A. Kramer

For my wife,

Judith Hahn Kramer

PEOPLE

Masters of the Universe

In shady alleys
behind black doors
predators wait
to steal with smiles,
promises, power point
fabricating profits,
borrowing thorough banks
the quarters and dollars
saved by working poor.
Playing hopscotch
with peoples' lives,
estates on lush lakes
suits bespoke on Bond Street,
a Rolls and a Rolex
executing merger documents
with Mont Blanc pens.
Their capped teeth
hiding pointed fangs,
masters of the universe
they style themselves
while others sweat
to repay their debts.

The Limo

A street, its sidewalks
littered with overdue bills
a line of tired men
waiting possible work
for one day, most
will be turned away hungry.
A limousine races past,
tinted windows, unseeable
mogul plotting strategy
on his laptop, cell phone
in hand whispering orders
to buy and sell at the opening.
It is seven thirty a.m.
a bitter wind rustles trash
lifting paper like kites
into the street, the limo
barely slows for a man
reeling across its path.
The chauffeur curses
his passenger oblivious.

Rubies and Doubloons

The pirates of imagination
trolling the seas for swag
wild with grog and shanties
ashore with flaming women
epitomes of freedom and wealth.
Today they hide in counting rooms
concocting ways to lighten
other people's wallets,
pinched little grey men,
Scrooge without the vision
of redemption. They troop
to Senate hearings not to
atone but to obfuscate,
not to confess but to confuse,
not to buckle or swash
but hide behind mumbled phrases.
There is no romance
in offshore banks
as there was in offshore chests
of gold and rubies and doubloons.

The Gingerbread Man

The gingerbread man
hops crossing the veldt
his right leg gnawed
by a cannibal king.
Keebler elves dance
nimble Jack jumps Jill
while dumpty humps
beside the parapet,
a masquerade ball
with fiddlers three
begun at half past ten.
Bread crumbs fill
the forest floor
marking the door
of the witch's home
the oven shut tightly
fattening pens cleared
and the grey man
strides the village green.

The Magician

The magician strides the stage
cape like a windless flag
black gloved, uttering tales
of the shadows of Cathay
Hindu Fakirs, voodoo
while a tiger paces, caged.
He will enter the enclosure
flash his cape and disappear
the tiger metamorphosized
into a spangled woman
but the cat, remembering
its time before imprisonment
leaps, slashing his throat.
The magic doused in blood.

The Evangelist

In a two thousand dollar suit,
bespoke from Bond Street
initialed shirts, Paisley tie from Paris
shoes crafted on his personal last
he strides to the altar, solemn smile
chin up tilted, outline ready
to deliver the words from God.
He is the idol of his flock
presenting their wool for him to wear.
He preaches the sermon from the Mount
of Mammon, cash is good
if you work hard, eye on the goal,
you care for your children, and me.
He never talks of Mother Theresa,
Father Damien or the doctor
trading organ solos for medicine.
His heroes are Carnegie, Mellon,
JP Morgan, sprinkling edifices
to lease a place in heaven
from a life of plunder and mansions.
He is the resurrected Christ,
St. Paul leading his people
into the land of scotch and chocolate.
When he returns après sermon
to his lavish estate
donning silk pajamas velvet robe
sliding into satin sheets
his dreams filled with Satan,
sweat seeps through his mattress.

The Race

Do they awake one day
and realize they are chosen
and gather bands of sycophants
and fly to Iowa, New Hampshire
rushing from diner to halls
of folding chairs, bunting draped
clutching microphones
salesmen selling words
intoned by rote, honed
by pollsters, authors
parsing phrases, catchwords
to raise the crowds to rise
applauding loudly, smile
capturing the moment
with nods of recognition.
What madness sends them out
from comfortable homes and beds
of silken sheets and pillows
to sleep, if sleep is possible,
in alien rooms, shoddy desks
execrable prints fixed to walls,
to rise and set the daily smile
countering the barbs of fellow seekers.
What madness drives them daily
a frightening wish for power
or for overweening rectitude?

Candidates

Like peddlers selling potions
from the backs of horse drawn wagons
elixirs for the bald, love for the loveless
nostrums, cure alls, wondrous potions.
They troop from town to city to hamlet
peddling themselves, promising change
from the drudgery of eeking daily bread
from jobs that might disappear, rabbits
in the hats of prestidigitators
phoning strangers for cash,
for their troops of sycophants,
so they can nibble cheesesteaks,
taste chitterlings, bratwurst
sip a beer demonstrating solidarity
with the common man, woman, voter.
But they will not be Andy Jackson
opening his home to muddy booted proles,
Lincoln finally pushed to righteousness.
They are power driven mortals
believing they are Messiah come
bearing universal cure for millenniums
of bigotry, cruelty, torture.
Scrutinized by members of the petty press,
pandering to prejudices, studying polls,
crafting words to move the souls
of those who would elect them king.

TV Newscasters

Besieged by pictures, words, faces
peddling the reconstructed old
or the vaguely new, we sit
immobile, ensconced in leather
watching a skewed or awful world
snippets of murder, robbery
tales of home invasion, tales
of killings fill quiet evenings
reality that is faked
contests where illiterates
demonstrate inadequate education.
We live solitary amid visions
amid would be leaders, needing
sound bites without substance
amid pundits spouting nonsense
amid calls to overmedicate.
How would it report the second coming
as a sporting event or as
a tale to be ignored?

Tycoon

Maturing in the oil fields,
coated in grease and sweat,
absorbing corporate lore,
obsessed with need
for power, wealth.
Supervisor, manager,
administrative assistant,
in middle age, President.
The company his family,
the odor of crude
always on his skin,
shedding people
despoiling the earth
the bottom line his god.
Devoid of charity
he will lie to save
his pile of stock,
wife and children meaningless,
sotted with importance
meeting after meeting,
a brief obit
in the Times
his final legacy.

The Cyclops

A cyclops keeps a unicorn
while centaurs and satyrs
roam the forests of its home.
A great dark castle
looming next the moat
the unicorn can leap
returning every night
to feed on sweet meats.
Shunned by human kind
the cyclops sits alone
pondering the universe
awaiting the leprechaun
invited guest for dinner,
cigars and brandy
by his blazing fireplace
discussing philosophy
and the failing of those
who rush in frantic gyres
to sublimate their fears.
Those tortured by age
the cyclops sees it all
enduring all in laughter.

The Bear and The Minstrel Man

The bear and the minstrel man
are dancing again, a quadrille
to whistling tracers,
the drumming bomb blasts
pock marking town squares,
the audience seated transfixed
hurls rocks and rotted peaches

The bear and the minstrel man
glower then laugh when their
backs are to the spectators.
They dare not wrestle
but paw the stage ground
with taloned feet hidden
beneath their trouser cuffs

The bear and the minstrel man
fascinating team in white face
sprinkling candy to the crowd
gathered far from the hall
dour men, drooling
craving sweets, laughing
at the agitated groundlings

Immigrants

They crossed the great divide
fearing death, but fearing more
the horrors they had left,
seeking peace or el dorado
in wagons, fetid boats
trains reeking of sweat.
Knaves or heroes they went
to places of rumor, of
towns built of mud
and there were others
dragged unwilling in shackles
indentured to pay their debts,
exiled for misdemeanors
enduring fists, whips
this nation of pioneers,
slaves and outcasts,
this nation of misfits.
This nation of Whitman's songs,
of patricians and poltroons
twice saved the world
forgoing conquest
and seeks to save the world
again.

Then Weep for Women

Like geese trotting the river bank
they wait to rent their bodies
for cash, for heroin and ecstasy
to dampen the sense of fetid flesh
pawing their breasts and thighs
or just for means to feed their kids.
We dare not ask what brought them
to that window in Amsterdam
that street, raising skirts, in Madrid
their roadside stance in Hungary
hailing truckers seeking coins
pacing their corner by the Lincoln Tunnel.
Myths spun by men of working girls
raped by uncles, cast out from slums
led away by cold eyed, slick voiced pimps
subjects of sociology students thesis
stolen to harems or fetid homes
trafficked from Third World shacks
offering anything in Port-au-Prince.
When will men endowed with humanity
offer a better way to feed
the bodies, minds, souls of women?

The Calm of Bacchus

The top of my brain
sprinkled with distilled barley
drifts ceilingward while
smoke drifts through my lips
and I am at peace, agitated
with the universe. Thank god
who gave us grape
to dampen pain of earth
and greed and tribes
desiring domination
over what ephemera
while my mind is off
and for an hour of smoke
and excessive scotch.
I am neither sad nor happy
but on a merry go round content
and I remember nothing,
want nothing, am nothing

A Modern Man

Behind his desk, enormous oak or teak
a leather chair cradling him
as he swivels from aide to phone
to computer screen, avid as a spider
moving those he's hired like chess pieces.
His corps of managers, accountants,
attorneys march to meetings to buy
to sell, to meet with investment bankers,
eager to hand him money raised
in various markets. Pocketing percentages
he dreams, tossing, of possible deals.
Visiting home and children between flights
on his private jet, he is the envy
of others, would be entrepreneurs,
who study his conquests in the Journal
covertly hoping one will fail.
Like the shark he lives in motion,
beyond wealth he needs the game.
When he seldom reads, it is biographies
of Carnegie, Mellon, Rockefeller.
Paintings brought him by dealers
line his walls, unseen, unstudied.
He relaxes, rarely, with a mistress
purchased at enormous price.
He lives in fear of death and poverty

Breaker Sateen

Breaker Sateen was a hell of a guy
he sat on his bunk and he thought with a sigh
I may be too old to do what I do.
Maybe its time to leave ship and leave crew.
Each day as I stretch and finally awake
I find that my legs increasingly ache
and when I sit down for a hurried first meal
I wonder how long I can stand how I feel.
Running this ship is both stressful and hard
caring for passengers for shipmates aboard
I love the horizon I cherish the sea
and wonder if after has meaning for me.
It's no fun to realize you're getting too old
to battle the waves and tolerate cold.
When your mind believes that you're still just a teen,
when you ponder the life and the man you have been,
but you know that at evening you suddenly tire,
and wonder if finally you're losing the fire
that led you to take to the onrushing ocean,
that led you to need its perpetual motion.
He knows much more now than when he began
but the wearing is tearing the job from the fun,
and he thinks if he chucks it and heads for the shore
will he get the same rush that he's gotten before.
When thinking of leaving he stifles a cry
like a fish on the beach he'll watch himself die.

An Encounter

Her father tenderly touched
the controls of the motorized chair
to which his daughter was meshed.
He had worked it from the van,
equipped to release the chair gently
with her strapped in, pavementward
to scoop her up when it was time.
Her legs were thin, atrophied, useless
and her hands deftly caressed the stick
turning her chair toward me
a stranger on a bench. I was relaxing
thinking thoughts of nothing.
Now studying her face, round,
like a balloon, plain, dressed plainly
her eyes seeking to see the place
to which she was transported.
I asked her, for want of better words,
how she was, unsure she could answer.
"Fine. I'm going to the game," she smiled.
Arena football, indoors, her first.
Her father stood protectively, mute.
She asked if I was going. "No
I am stopping here one day,
to see her city and leave for the next,"
I prated. She told me to drive carefully,
said "I'll pray for you" and slowly
drove off, her father patting her shoulder.

The Funeral

In the hot and dimmed room
row on row of mourners
some with tears oozing
some granite pursed mouths
some joking, some silent
the rabbi, the cantor
stride out of their study
performing service by rote
the dirge, *el moley rachamim*
the obligatory ditty of life
with death its destination
and then the eulogy, euphemisms
"a man of strength" rather
than hateful bastard
a good provider rather
than greedy momzer
and finally all must stand
recite the Mourners Kaddish
and wheel the coffin out
to the hearse, to plant
leaving the children
to fight for their spoils

Ghosts

Dylan Thomas

1. In undershorts, mad
   with drink, raving
   as only poets rave
   and asking me to pimp
   for him in a town
   without women
   he spoke, got his fee
   and drifted on to die.

Elizabeth B.

2. She parceled out the dregs
   of her inheritance
   this bit for food
   a bit for hose, so much
   to heat the estate, crumbling
   evidence of her lineage
   of financiers, doyens.
   She could have sold the home
   lived her last years in comfort
   but alone, with family portraits
   dressed in fading black
   she sought me out to save
   her home from government
   bringing progress, sewers
   for her to buy. She found me
   a boy believing an author
   could work a miracle.
   I did, having no one else to help.
   Her obituary mentioned the home
   an old woman living alone
   scion of an old and wealthy past

nothing of her faded black dress
or how she almost lost her pride.

Milton Simms Kramer

3. His eyes analyzed from organs to skin
   dark alert eyes, black shaven beard
   he was older, speaking powerfully,
   when my voice cracked past puberty.
   Brilliant yet followed by others.
   We spoke of partnership
   knowing it was just banter
   for he could own the world
   and me barely myself.
   He died before he lived
   leaving me to partner alone.

Sam Kesselman

4. He was my father's legacy
   dumped on me to salvage funds
   improvidently handed a stranger.
   He was a visionary
   creating homes, solid, lovely
   forgetting costs to make it right.
   He was partner and friend
   and near his end describing
   pain, dialysis of the disease
   I never had, speaking simply
   dying gracefully smiling.

Howard Simons

5. Born gentle, whose diabetes
   as it flared to amputation,
   turned angry at home.
   He did not speak of pain

keeping his affliction secret
until it bubbled out
and he acknowledged all.
A healer incapable
of healing himself,
his heart rebelling
like cards dealt, flashed,
he showed his hand and died.

Herb Salus

6. The kindest and cruelest man
   screaming at ill perceived slights
   as his brain boiled, then
   suddenly repentant.
   Suit rumpled, round faced
   threatening suicide
   so he could be calmed.
   He counseled wisely
   depressive rarely manic.
   Death took him gently
   his kind heart took him
   sitting a book at his lap.
   The cruelest of obituaries
   the vultures of the press
   never knew him as did
   the throng at his funeral.

   JAY

7. He died cruelly, thrashing
   pierced with tubes, bubbling
   his elegance of movement gone
   the easy smile twisted
   his face a knotted rope,
   in life dancing always
   at the edge of the precipice.

He planned his death carefully
unlike his life, pouring alcohol
on a diseased liver, justifying impropriety
supremely kind to friends, the young
brilliant but unwise, a Pierrot
joking through constant pain
a broiling pile of contradiction
tending his children, as a horticulturist
nurturing and breeding roses.
All watched when he danced
an amateur Astaire
who stumbled only as he lived.

Italo Scanga

8. An army of fear and ambiguity
   creatures of his frenetic soul
   seeking twisted branches
   trunks of olive wood
   obsessed with resurrection
   child of ancient and new lands.
   He left a legacy of weird
   and wonderful imaginings
   melding paint and sculpture
   a body hard as granite
   a mind frantic and defensive
   he filled his world with silence

John Ahern

9. A rumpled man of faith
    I watched him turn to stone
    years ago, rigid mute
    eyes staring in horror
    he lived. We spoke of history
    philosophy, never religion.
    I learned today he died
    I shall see him once in death
    and now he knows
    standing beside his god
    or was it only myth.

Jamie Moyer — Pitcher

His motion like lava oozing downhill,
thirty years sanding his craft.
Professional commentators
who never threw a ball toward
a batter focused on his arm,
pontificate he throws junk
when kids are getting battered
with ninety six mile per pitches,
He hits spots, inside corner
out at the knees, change up
sinker – all the same motion.
Watching him is like Nureyev
motion seemingly artless
knowledge of the trade buried
unseen in his mind.

Madoff

At what instant, what epiphany,
did he change from charlatan
to thief? Believing his formula
of wealth his vast knowledge
his magical insight, when?
What little error morphed him
creating profit from air
knowing he could recoup
as the dollars, euros, dinars
arrived in bulk, he,
overwhelmed, let it stand
his mind in stasis, unable
to construct a modern model
with an aging brain
paying from the endless horde,
money he could not earn.
Lavishing charity, trapped
in his life, he could not fold
his cards and walk away.
At what instant did he know
his fame would eclipse Ponzi?

Maurice

He comes each month
with canisters of poison
to dam the swarm of insects
seeking warmth. They owned
the land our home captured.
Spraying baseboards quickly
speeding from house to house.
A nomad by day, a Hessian
returning home each night
to wife to child to dinner
and before sunrise again
out to protect or ravage.

Eulogy to Mr. Kimble

He will never come again
unannounced into my office
settling his bulk
across my desk
reassured I am still there
in his dark suit
pressed against his dark skin.
We will never speak of families.
He knew I knew his past
dead wife, dead daughter
the crime of his youth
we never spoke of those
we did not have to reminisce
we spoke of now and future
and now there is no future.
I will no longer hand him
a cigar, his last one
a wand in his huge hand
in his wooden casket.
He layed there, not him
a waxen lifeless figure
the resonant voice gone
the massive body shrunken
this friend of my youth
friend of my olding age.

PLACES

What's Good For America

Highways, graceful parabolas
like a seven layer cake
promising unencumbered movement
from into and out of place.
The miniature autos racing
the diorama, while I sat.
Circling in wonder the future
that would be delayed by war
but I was a child, safe.
Years later I saw the reality
of that expansive construct,
cities clogged with oxygen defiled
workers miles from Levitt's homes
escapees from crumbling cities
working ceding hours driving
to and from their tiny plots
while lobbyists whispered
build roads to willing pols
and the corporation fattened.
What's good for GM is good
for America, a mantra,
live large build large
elephantiasis in transportation.
Mired in the quicksand of past
those geniuses of industry
scorned miniaturization in Asia
ignored the plotting of OPEC
denied the rising of the waters
forgot the teaching of the dinosaurs,
consumed with hubris and greed.
It too has withered, dying
the Pavilion disassembled
its vision our reality
of unintended consequences.

The Wild West

A gas station, pumps gone
grocery empty shelves, crumpled
houses uniformly grey, pitted
from decades of sand blown
down the lone street, wind
stripped the walls of paint.
One saguaro cactus stands
by the cracked welcome sign
the town's name obliterated
the silver mine played out
the wells went dry one summer
when there was no rain, children
had already escaped the tedium
the old ones lay under flattened stones
or drifted to the city to die.
The town waits, plumbing stripped
whatever was salvageable gone
a breakwater for the wind
a place devoid of memory.

Tombstone

Bones of the gunmen
in slanted graves – Boot Hill
a stroll from the bar room
the oomphalus of America.
Cut outs denoting death,
blasting tapes of six guns
a recurring sound track,
post-packaged good and evil
the jury of the holster
(neighbors battered a rapist yesterday).

Wyatt and the consumptive doctor
like figures on Rushmore
the tamped dirt floor
the wooden fence (Sawyer)
the sweet hint of blood
encapsulated in the town
(The dance hall girls waitressing
the smoke house, tourists)
that would not die
surviving on memories of murder
(a figure in military Mufti
astride a sleek carrier
shouts "bring it on").

Post Cards

I Nassau

> I met him first, blind
> guided by a slim boy
> pencil fingers caressing
> strings, birthing the rhythm
> songs of the island
> his voice, a river bounding rocks.
> I learned his lilt
> seeking the calm of Nassau
> before the many tourists
> before the casinos
> before the hucksters
> he sung of silent beaches
> sung of laughter.
> I saw him years later
> his trio behind a rope,
> become an organ grinder's monkey
> a background for tourists
> the voice almost monotone
> muzak for island women
> impressed to pass out flyers
> for liquor and jewelry shops
> the Junkeneau parade.
> Once joyous, ragtag marchers
> now a scripted show
> for Hawaiian shirted tourists
> off monstrous cruise ships
> strolling shop filled streets
> the beat of flip flops
> supplanting the gentle drums
> the liquid strumming
> of Blake's guitar.

II Custer State Park

    Clueless, I parked my car
    close to the herd
    walked nearing the bull
    protector of his bison.
    He pawed earth snorting
    we stared, each at each
    and I glanced past
    at the swath of forest
    trees, bushes felled.
    a road, made just before
    I came. They grazed
    the field where he and I
    eyed the other, an eternity
    until I strolled back
    drove to the inn
    where they warned of danger
    I endured. But I
    had had no fear
    having lived in wonder.

III Puerto Rico

    The groom dressed in uniform
    a gilded costume like a wooden soldier
    of the nutcracker. The bride
    beautiful in white,
    I was asked to dance with her,
    I, the celebrity from the west,
    I, almost a boy, sent
    to keep the pickers safe,
    to school their children,
    to meet the island's saint.
    Berdecea too soon dead
    creator of legends
    a man from dirt to power

remembering his childhood
to wisely help his citizens.
Those several days
lunches with mayors
political conversation
I learned a vibrant people
our people called spics.

IV Haiti

Lounging at the villa's pool
languidly sensing lush wooded hills
poverty would soon turn to dirt.
Discussing philosophy with men
educated in Paris their walls
studded with vibrant oils,
but the pool tender's home
is a webbed lounger.
The poet asked me for a weekend trip
he thought me gay, I thought
his poems weak. This poor land,
fear engendered by Tontin McCoudies,
fear of witches, of Papa Doc
repressing his Hippocratic oath,
to steal the last bit
of his impoverished nation.
After sunset, dirt packed floor,
a roof, open sides,
a voodoo temple
unadorned, drums only.
A covey of teenaged girls
dressed in white, a ceremony
to induce the gods to
find them decent jobs.
The drums beat monotonously
as the preacher importunes heaven,
the children march out

a seeming old woman
dressed in black, mourning
for her youth, a child, her land
a husband dead or gone,
screams, drops to ground
rolling, spittle at her lips
speaking unknown tongues
reaching the roof support,
she is rolled back to center.
The drums louder, louder
Jesus statue on a post
a Mona Lisa smile
the woman's pitch rises.
I am a solitary stranger
comprehending almost nothing.
A rooster is brought, displayed.
I leave to return to the villa
my taxi stops for gas
enough for the trip back.

V New Orleans

    Wrought iron filigree
    guarding second story balconies
    wondrous to the tot I was
    hearing streets of music.
    Survivor of underwater gasping
    I laughed at the singer
    at the puppet show
    almost secure in the city.
    Seventeen years later
    southernmost stop on our
    trip through America
    savoring beignets and Po Boys
    and chicory coffee
    with the laughing debutante
    I'd met in the park.

This city of contradictions,
the dead lie above ground
while tourists wobbling
down Bourbon Street
downing beer in plastic
topple asleep in mud,
the band plays The Saints
Didn't He Ramble
wheeling the coffin
to the tomb and then
the party to honor the dead
with booze and brass.
This city made a president
in battle après the war.
Seven years later
I brought my bride
to my remembered hotel
now somewhat seedy,
to the restaurant
where Napoleon's bell
was sounded with brandy
where we laughed
at our Mexican souvenirs
and stood in Preservation Hall
preserved by our homies
and listened to old men
playing real jazz.
And years later
came to litigate,
we Don Quixotes
against the wooden giants
and while my partners
embraced the city's charms
I sat eating dinner
alone in the Royal Sonesta
entranced by the tale
of capture and slavery

the parents of musicians
made oxen in our grand nation.
They have destroyed
my second city with
storm and flood and oil
but it will rise again
with Saints and Mardi Gras
the music cannot die.

Return

I shall, must, return to Paris
obsessed with the calming scent
of fresh baked croissants, watching
bocci on the Luxembourg Gardens
wandering the ancient Louvre corridors
home to Rembrandt, David, Michelangelo,
beginning the climb to Winged Victory.
I know these steps, these rooms
the great hall, on the left,
only in France the marble hermaphrodite
rounded breasts like peaches
intact penis – repulsion, desire
dream or portrait, life from stone
the modeling is perfect, symmetrical.
I pass glancing the Mona Lisa
symbol of hype trumping performance
finally, high up the wall, the vagina
perfect, a glowing rose
yang to the sculpture's yin.
I will exit, walk the boulevards
lunch on croque masseur and wine
regaining youth in that aged city.

Centralia

Fire deep in earth's entrails
unquenchable, decade on decade
slowly eating the seam,
a dragon stretching to escape
its prison of rock. Its fumes
have wasted that tiny town
engendering intimations of Hell
odor of brimstone
fume geysers leeching upward
abandoned streets turning
mud. Where are the flowers?
Prometheus blessing turned curse
and still unseen it burns
and in that burning stench
the flames of Buchenwald remembered
the auto de fé for the maid
the piles of human bones.
We must build a shrine
in Centralia to nature
an eternal flame
borne high by a statue
of a man in chains.

Haiti

The fire in the fields
and in the eyes of men
gone mad for warmth,
intonations of the preacher,
beat of the drums,
mushroom visions,
the screech of the chicken
writhing the dirt floor,
unintelligible syllables
passion in a hopeless land.
This once green place
of rolling hills
children schooled in Paris,
men discussing philosophy
after hospital rounds.
Now women offer their babies
to strangers, tourists,
those few seeking exotica
or viewing poverty
like etymologists.
A nation stripped of pride
by the neurosis and greed
of vicious rulers.

El Camino Real

The road, bearing semis
carrying artichokes
steel rods, legends
of Spain, visions
of helmeted conquistadors
leading dour proselytizers
to enslave the people with their
crucified god. Now a street
with paint peeling motels
laundromats, big boy burgers.
Ghosts patrol this concrete
drifting tattoo parlors
still seeking el dorado
in store front churches.
I see these displaced shades
hear their questioning
smell the ashes of their graves.

Yalta

At a small table, in a modest room
a dying man, a monster, a genius
together with their minions played,
tossing a million lives here,
a city there, people, places
they never knew, a high stakes game
betting with other people's goods.
They rested comfortable in soft beds
courtiers praising their wisdom,
fine food and wine,
a photograph of three smiling faces
published to circle the globe.

In Roumania

Derricks like huge giraffes
stand idle on the docks
awaiting prosperity, to find
this nation ravaged by a ruler
believing himself immortal,
believing himself loved, feared.
He met Vlad in hell, laughing
"better to impale than be impaled,"
whispered his mouth above
the vat of boiling oil.
This is a land of cannibals
devouring its gypsies, its Jews
while eaten by hungry neighbors.
A nation of cracked roads
crumbling sidewalks
dust filled museums,
homages to departed conquerors
parks strewn with roman flotsam.
Flowers grow pale here
unkempt dogs, scrawny, limp
the streets hunting scraps.
No one notices or pets them,
this is a bleak and ruined land.

Normandy

White stone, rows of white
crosses, stars, sunlight
dancing off the near bay
rotting hulks of rafts
rotting bones of youth
this place destined by madness
to be built of blood and skin.
When words can turn men rabid
this place where Satan dances
this place where mothers weep.

Israel

They have built a tiny enclave
part garden, part fortress
to shelter the remnant from those
who would kill each one
and be left without scapegoats
for their failures, for their sins.
The walking dead. The very few,
models for Giacometti
who came to that barren land
of trees planted with pennies
and with dimes squirreled in boxes,
blue as Hebrew's sky,
of rifles bought with dollars
harvested from merchants
atoning for the sin of parents
who escaped soon enough.
And when their neighbors attacked,
the imminent final solution,
the remnant no longer passive.
Thermopoli with planes wheeling
now east, now west
the very few become an armada
improbable victory of necessity
and then to fight again
and fight again and build
a land of scholars where
each man, each woman a soldier.
Professors, doctors, farmers
learning the terrible art of war.
This is the strangest land
where wounded enemies are brought
to their hospitals to heal,
where farms are planted
beneath enemy fortifications,

where mosques are guarded
by those reviled by worshippers.
They would flower their neighbor's lands
if only left to live in peace.

Haunted House

That great and fading house
façade melting like a paraffin mask
on the equator. Built by a merchant,
a mansion for the generations
of children he never sired.
The sturdy walls are cracked
strands of lathe and powdered plaster
visible between peeling lead paint patches.
The bedroom doors are either gone
or lying athwart their hinges,
the copper pipes, prey of vandals
sold years ago as scrap.
There are footsteps on the ceiling
painted by children chasing rumors
of sounds in a haunted house.
Once tailored gardens stand
a farm for weeds and brambles.
The house will be rebuilt
its grounds weeded and planted
with roses and peach trees,
fitted for others descendants

Tenement

Wash hanging out second story window
flecked with carbon particulates,
a cracked flower pot sans flower,
brick spotted with faded paint,
broken chair shoved at the wall,
next a child's scooter wheel lost.
A man, unemployed, out a window
peers at children at the corner.
How many live in this ancient tenement
working through dusk for the landlord
who lives with a washing machine
past close-cut suburban lawns

Two Poems of No Connection

I Nassau

    Like a Chinese dragon
    new year with firecrackers
    and bowls of brown rice,
    dancing down the road
    my city's Mummers with poor
    ragged floats, patched costumes
    dancing joyously like children.
    The drums, guitars
    Blind Blake younger
    Adam and Eve cavorting
    gaping tourists rum sotted
    on tails of dragons,
    imagining the bronze women
    laughing at the curbs
    noticing the jewelry shops
    winking lascivious smiles,
    swaying to the drum beats
    and steel drum music
    untouchable to those men
    off the cruise ship
    with pasty skin and bellies,
    padded in sirloin and onion rings.
    Awaiting their lithe lovers
    stripped of soiled costumes
    in hats at city's edge
    and I, watching them return
    on little dories to the ship,
    return to my hotel room
    awaiting the morning, the walk
    down the littered road
    to continental breakfast.
    Another morning in sun

when I alone can contemplate
the shape of clouds
the slurping of the waves
the cobbled path of life.

II At Home

Like a spider, staring
down his web, its kingdom
created magically from its flesh
I sit enfolded in leather,
a high backed chair
a desk of polished teak
one phone, one computer
all roads lead away
from my miniscule empire,
to those seeking solace
advice, assurance of justice
in a world of chance.
Life is fragile,
memory short lived
separated from death
by luck, by a single moment
of place, of time, of space.
We are pushed, screaming
into the unknown
safety gone, certainty
a bog of quicksand.
We are sucked into time
to ponder the unknowable
questions always asked
until fateful darkness
cloaks us in fateful answers.

Things in Nature

To The Sea

The river formed of springs
bubbling like shaken soda
from rock encrusted soil
merged with melting ice
from the treeless mountains
flows ambling gentle slopes
to the first cataract, spume
like a fierce forest fire
fogs sight, engenders terror.
Only the wisest can navigate
the river rimmed with an array
of candles, extinguished
one by one by breezes,
only the bravest can ride
beneath gnarled branches
down the narrow waterfalls
around bends, imps appear
leering with green teeth
purple eyes, fingernails
like sabers. There a hut
built of driftwood, winds
then drifting calmly past
summer cottages where wealthy
clip their toenails and coupons,
watching leaves floating slowly
to the unseen second cataract
then in a rush past high rising
offices, apartment buildings.
The city waking at dawn
commuters oblivious to water
past docks, ships holds
filled with goods for export
then meshing with the ocean
where ancient vessels rot
unseen, unknown at the floor.

The Ant

Is there a sentient being
in that tiny black speck
scurrying grass stalks
back to its nurturing hive
bypassing a rotting branch
crawling a brown fallen leaf.
Was it born to luxury
or on the crew that dug
and built the tribal home?
Does it pray each morning
that a booted monster
will refrain from crushing it?

The Cat

I sing a song for the cat that is not,
for the mouser who's here and suddenly gone,
for the god of Bobastis is the pet of the witch.
Of rich dappled fur, metaphorical tail
that can dance with delight or presage a bite
on the wrist of the one who lavishes food,
in payment for watching its lithe silken pace
that a leaf in a breeze would be jealous of.
It brings me a gift, a chipmunk or grape,
awaiting expressions of parallel love
or fear or awe as its patriarchs knew
in their home by the Nile as present day tigers
are wont to engender, as cheetahs
that race with the storm have received.
But it sits and it stares to be scratched
on that spot near its ears that it bears
while sitting then scampering into the wild
in hunt for a bird or a rabbit or water.
To stride to its home when ready for warmth
or a morsel of catnip or herring in sauce,
one cannot tell if it's happy or sad,
one cannot tell if it's hunter or tamed,
but we know that the cat is very like us.

The Shark

Like the start of freshman
tug of war, yanked forward
strain back at the fish
too far to see. It charged the ship
reeling fast 'til my wrists numbed
working the rod back, forward,
keeping the line taut as it came
fin cutting the ocean
charging the boat like a bull
after a waving cape, all fury.
Palms aching holding the rod
it was big and gaffed
it thrashed as the Pacific
turned pink. Boated on the gaffe
it writhed on the deck and died
a thing too beautiful to kill
grey and tiger wild. I could not
take it lifeless. A gift
for the crew to feast
and I would never fish again.

Rock Garden

Grown through a crack in the north face
of the mountain, the sheer rock escarpment,
a flower, velvet petals, lilac stem
black as if enamel had been fired
on sheets of coal, lustrous
the suns' dark twin,
solitary on its cliff, smooth
as if sanded by the gods
created as the center of the centerpiece
for the feast of creation

The Azaleas Bloom

The azaleas bloom fire red
a field of passion bright
next the pruned rose sticks
that may bud in time — red
abutting brown, abutting grass
a masterwork, a Rothko
but stronger of deeper hue
of resurrection after winter
that bombarded earth with snow
crushing bushes, rending limbs
of spruce and oak.
The azaleas survived
more lovely than remembered.

MAZE

Bushes higher than sight
trudging damp paths to exit
returning again and once again
to the same copse blocking
I am lost in vertigo
to claustrophobia lost.
I brush the knobby branches
scrape my arm, terror
like boiling oil searing me.
I see a man free
above the maze entowered.
Will he point the way
for me to extricate me
before I leap impaling me
on brambles or fly
like Daedelus to death.

The Rose

Encased in silken folds of purest red
overpowering aroma of sweet earth
atop untouchable nest of thorns,
a rose is heaven's gift to man.
It blooms wild in fields of weeds
oasis from bees and butterflies,
a symbol of perfect peace.
Yet men waged war
in its name, humankind tramples
every treasure given it.

Hours of Amazement

In time we saw the lights
glowing embers in a sea of clouds
and wondered at the wonder
of cotton balls in Brownian dance,
an exploding sky, July fireworks
Father Christmas night in Nancy.
Our souls floating toward heaven
merging celestial ballet
we waltz with Venus watching Mars
dance the Fandango with angels
in white chiffon flowing gowns
our frantic hour of earthly joy.

There are hours of amazement
times we truly see inside
and outside of other minds
sensing the pulsing core of earth,
feel ice embedded clouds
and hear a solitary cricket
rubbing its legs in exultation.
These are the hours of maniacs
these are the moments of death,
when is seen a great light
a sudden rush of silence.

Warm October

I am suffused in the light
of a warm October sun
an unexpected gift
wind blowing easily
as if to gentle
the fall of maple leaves.
Sunday entered quietly
without a wakening alarm
and we tasted omelets
crisp bacon and muffins,
we joked easily skipping
the articles of horror.
A day to repress thoughts
of the world's atrocities
and drift the hours
like a paddleless canoe
floating a tranquil lake.

Fall Descends

The geese are flying south
the annual striptease of trees
clouds thicken, a smell of snow
impending fills my lungs,
squirrels in frantic dance
climb down gathering nuts
to store against the future cold.
The last days of October,
beaches empty of summer's tourists
night comes too early,
we hoard frozen dinners
to tide us over until spring.

First Snow

The few remaining leaves
are tipped in flakes
of snow,
wind now gusting
now quiescent, the earth
is white, a bride standing
before entering her aisle,
neither footprints
nor deer prints yet.
No soot, exhaust tracks
or tree limbs to mar
perfect white.
First snow fall,
a gentle chill
all trade has ceased
sleds refound in closets.
It will be time for
angels in the snow,
for yellow Christmas lights,
for children laughing
big in mackinaws and boots
and trooping out
with snowball armament
to learn the strategies of war.

The Earth Like Diamonds

The ice storm bloomed
diamonds in the grass
evergreens already lighted
for Christmas, sky slashed
with sun white clouds,
a gigantic V the after image
left by geese migration,
the sun echoes off pellets
beads of purest crystal
bushes frozen still silent,
there is a sacred quiet
no wind no intimation of men.

Philadelphia

Philadelphia Then

With the eyes of a ewe
in grey sack dress
arm pits hairy
round as a canister
she stands mute
cup outstanding
for coins of strangers.
Every day in place
like a wishing well for
men of commerce and law.
She is a priestess
of silent absolution
seeking offerings
of pocket change.

Down the next street
barks duck-voiced
a woman, eyes agape,
leaps auto hoods
stops morning traffic
a crackling warning
she is our oracle.

The major is welcomed
tiny, uniformed
she marches the courthouse
from chamber to chamber
gathering contributions
for her unknown cause.

I was so very young,
life unwritten pages
in a land of mystery
calmly debating fate

of the day's parade
of possible felons
freedom or jail
over glasses of rye
with the final arbiter
who paid daily tribute
for the power handed him.
Power over life and death
power to forgive
or righteous wrath
to slam the prison gates.

Down Market Street

Clanging in the night
of harness strap and bells
on the trap moving easy
the cobblestones
down Market Street
past Ben's Print Shop
and the new made house
upending the weiner stand.
The tired plug trots
with tourists from some
midwest town laughing,
a moth worn blanket
shielding the wind,
past buildings where giants
plotted unknowable futures
debating phrases so that
Delaware could stand with
Pennsylvania. Ride past
the alley father, son, holy ghost,
past Christ's Church and
Solomon's house of worship
and where the seamstress
may have made the flag,
past the unringing bell
which some say will chime
with the clarity of heaven
when peace and brotherhood emerge
from the fractious minds of men.

The Club

A room for plump Victorians
of dark panel and dim lights,
portraits of pursed lip men
balled fists, frog eyes,
a Christmas tree lonely
in a far corner, a star
for a hat, dressed in tinsel
a dead thing ringed by pictures
of long dead industrialists
forgotten names, forgotten deeds.
Tinkerbell would die
entering this room
dusted by downcast servants
shrinking from staring eyes
ringing muted walls.
A piercing ambulance siren
penetrates these thick walls,
a room devoid of laughter
in a building out of time.

A Walk on Market Street

A man, jugged and wasted,
a Giacometti sculpture
sits on the ledge of a wall
stares at nothing, ewe eyes,
smiles when a walker looks at him
without pity or repugnance.
A one legged man
spins on metal crutches
to greet tourists
with outstretched paper cup
begging coins with the rasp of a crow.
The grinding sound of the door
of a panel truck being raised,
the fat smell of corned beef,
a policeman drives the street
glancing from his cardboard cup
filled with coffee to scout crime.
The suits march purposely
from board rooms and courtrooms
to their gated court townhouses
and one acre mini mansions.
Pinstripes rep ties
red and blue whether or not
they graduated Penn.
There are vacant stores
where people sat over cinnamon buns,
a low end mall where Leary's
had the Declaration, uninventoried.
Gimbels and Strawbridges
strode the cobbled sidewalk
where horse drawn carriages
rode and where they ride.
Rap blares from a shop, a place
that Jefferson and Franklin passed,

soiled papers blown in gutters
of the street where the great bell
rang and cracked, where liberty
was proclaimed for some, but not
for ancestors of the beggars.

I enter a dark foyer
descend steps to the station
buried under Chestnut Street,
the train arrives with a noise
like the whoosh of a steam engine,
the odor of lubricating oil
wafts from below the wall
of tiles in abstract array,
varicolored of greens and yellows
reds, oranges and whites
they climb the wall diagonal.
I sit, the platform fills
a woman, fat as a sow,
plops next me bumping me
no apology, perhaps she is mute
or incapable of feeling.
I move to use my cell phone
to reconnect with the upper world.

For Charity

The refurbishing temple of God facing
toward back-passing men
mute with morning rum, glancing
at the new scrubbed structure.
There I pondered fate and
learned the virtues of bourbon.
A place, now gone, where my father
sipping coffee with my young me
chatted with Moore, impeccably clothed
cursed by black, defender of thieves
at fifty bucks a pop, I laughed
as they tossed tales like raindrops.
Two mad men, one on scotch
and one on inborn humors.
I strolled toward Napoleon
to join the party where couples
in bespoke suits and branded frocks
ate filet mignon for the poor.

Personal Musings

Tales of My Father

Unlike Samson his strength was in his eyes
piercing in thought, soft when the humors
embedded him. When his barber's hands,
sliced by the shattering light globe
shook, he endured nicks daily.
Like a matador, briefcase fluttering
distracting onrushing automobiles
until the men in blue, seeing him
stopped traffic as for a blind prince.
He told stories, holding strangers
rapt hours on the train south
or toastmaster to charities.
He bore the title to his book
he never wrote, a mantra.
His energy pulsed and waned.
As author, as politico
conception not completion.
He charmed the jury
as he must have early
charmed his wife.
Wit and passion
tipped with madness.
The weeks after the crash
lying healing unable to walk
working only the phones
may have been his best,
better than stroke crippled
unable to lift a fork
puffing a Dutch Master
his only lasting pleasure,
better than his brilliance blasted
by barbarous treatment
culled from the dark ages,
better than rarely sated passions

the times of screaming rage,
better than the time of fear
threatened if he should lose
as the world and his body
turned against him as the church
denouncing a heretic.
He never bragged about himself
was always gentle to his wife
and to the old woman.
Frustrations visited on the son
he loved too much to say.

The Velvet Suit

The suit was cut and sewn
with care and love beyond
any tailor's, beyond tenderness
of muted velvet, an angora cat
to the touch, buttons rich
shells, its fit perfection.
I was a prince that morning
when Grandma presented it.
I dressed myself, halting
each moment to caress a sleeve
buttoning the jacket and peeking
several times at the mirror
to see me new blooming,
a purple butterfly
striding into school
my first day, first grade.
My classmates interrupted class
over and over to touch
my sleeves and laugh.
I thought not happiness
for me but at me
for acting the snob.
I came home weeping
and never wore the suit again

Childhood

We ran the back alley
where the milkman came silent
and the grocery man sang
his wares, oranges, chopped meat.
And we rode our bikes
down to the truck farm
where the big streets crossed,
and past the forest where
trash was surreptitiously dumped,
and we ran away to live there
till night with no stars
and the whimpering of rats
tasting the garbage, yellow eyed
and, we were told, bearers of death.
We lived in fear of polio
that came from public pools.
We lived in warnings and in terror.
Our school was built off plans
designed for prisons and modified
enlarging cells to class rooms.
We played in asphalt yards
box ball and dodge ball while girls
jumped rope and tittered gossip.
And I knew they laughed at me
at my glasses and my books.

Battles of Childhood

Hiding behind stones our pretended mountains
pushing our men of lead, our tanks, our cannon
through the sparse unhiding whisps of grass
digging trenches, underground redoubts
where some still wait the battle's end.
We counted casualties of our creation,
We packed our troops in paper bags
to separate for dinner, having planned
our next weeks skirmish in a war
that never ended. Two little boys
mimicking the world our parents made.
I glued a world map to my bedroom wall
sticking colored pins in places read about
in each day's news, each morning's horror
and barely understood that was not play.
Years later another friend, a school mate,
told me of his father's death, Bataan.
My pin had marked that place that march.
When I was grown, embedded in mud
practicing killing with my weapon
recoiling painful at my shoulder,
I recalled the pins and prayed
that I would not become a doll
pierced by voodoo priestess juju
as a chicken twirled and dashed.

First Day

I slowly walked across the bridge
joining New Hampshire, Vermont
withholding tears, gazing down
the river, contemplating fear
of leaping the banister.
I had been away from home
often but not like this
abandoned in a friendless place
staring at the solitary moon
contemplating years of solitude
my mind roiling contradiction
to run, to stop, to return.
Finding the mountains in shadow
formed by receding ice
formed of granite, symbol
of what I must become,
reformed craving silence
so ungrown, unsure
so sure of failure.
I glanced the moon
cold as I was cold
and walked across
state to state
farms, grass, water.
I was of the city
I was alive, exiled
with those who learned
wisdom in prep schools
I had never heard of,
homes I had never visited
calm I had never experienced.

Placed with a boy
in one room, claustrophobic,

whom I could only tolerate.
We were able to speak reality
later, only that last night
we would live together
when I finally discovered
I was not a mutant freak,
long after my silent walk.

My Study

I am content in my study
lined with books gathered a lifetime
four marvelous, strange paintings
a dreamscape, a snake
slithering upward to pink sky
butterflies or pine cones
a leafless tree, an abstract frame.
Custer, pierced as Saint Sebastian
against a darkening sky
black clouds, a man bound
erect. Christ-like face
a frame within a frame
and the twin portraits
Jacob, muscles straining
bearded, eyes world weary
dreaming the ladder, angels
and then embracing an angel
wrestling as two leaves
come together in September falling.
The books, the world brought home.

Poems Are Pessimistic

Poems are pessimistic
a rose is a rose is a rose
says nothing of the touch
the velvet scented touch
of the richest flower
its blooming summer's apex.
We speak of withering age
the fearsome fact of death
we see a world of cruelty
the martyrdom of saints,
Dante descending hell
to find his muse
the valley of the shadow
pervades our shadowed words.
Etherized patients inhabit
our sorry pages, we stare
walking trash strewn streets
viewing the ball through piles
of dead corsages.
Blue moons moan
for love is always lost
and laughter fleeting,
we write of bodies piled
like kindling, cremation
of the soul, withering
ancient flesh, children
starving at the margins
of killing field, orphaned
by men nurtured in hate.
Depression sometimes lifts
in visions of clouds, stars
but in the end the words
are ink on paper signifying nothing.

Superbowl Sunday

The city will be still tonight
streets devoid of muggers
restaurants empty, sports bars
filled with cheers of men
swilling beer from pitchers
chomping chips with salsa
cheering their team to win
or even cover the spread.
How many millions will be bet
on Patriots, Giants
grappling for the golden rings.
Whose career will end in pain
which coach doused in Gatorade.
Champagne will flow tonight
in Boston or New York
in Vegas cash will flow like
water inundating New Orleans
Candidates, speechless,
will watch with friends,
Friends gather at parties
a nation unified
rapt watching television
seeking new found heroes
to go to Disneyland.

A Game of Golf

"Wasn't that the worst thing ever,"
she said, through her mouth,
lines erased by surgery,
pressed golf shirt carrying
a matched set of Ping irons.
"What," I asked, "was so terrible?"
"How slow the foursome was
ahead of us." "No," I said
"the worst thing is what is happening
in Darfur." "Oh get serious"
she sneered. I walked away.

After Christmas

Clouds seem cast
like gunpowder grey sheets
across the fading lights
of a winter afternoon.
Past the solstice, past
Christmas, when depression
lessens slightly for the lonely,
and some decorations are stored,
and some left hanging
on living conifers
and sidewalks store
shedding pines for trash.
Frantic new year parties
are days ahead
with hope for better days
hopeless resolutions
as if the earth and we
will be new born,
different, a diapered cliché.
Losing ourselves in whiskey,
wishing, praying for magic,
as night mutes celebration.
Who will live, who die
in the glorious year
to come?

An Old and Soggy Tale

There is an old and soggy tale
of a man alone in a ship of sails
who, leaving port, determined to go on
until he saw the whole of earth
or died. He wrote of mammoth dragons
swimming while waves doused their fire,
mermaids pouting lecherously for him
and tiny people, each with two heads,
who rowed to him with gifts of food.
He wrote of lands of ice and lands
where wine poured free from wells.
He wrote of lives well lived
and people hunched in fear.
He wrote that he had found the way
and set it down, a map to peace.
They found his diary, and burned it.

PHILOSOPHY

The Seven Deadly Sins

Lust

    Staring at Uriah's wife, naked
    breasts, honeydews rose tipped
    feeling a tickle at his scrotum,
    David, glancing away, eyes returned
    to the woman created for a king
    earned that slingshot afternoon.
    Women want the brave, the tender
    crooner of psalms to heaven, silk mouthed,
    the body of a whippet. He must have her
    if her husband dies by chance.
    As spotter for the army,
    the odds of a fly fixed in a web.
    He slept haltingly waiting the time
    when he could comfort and possess
    to finally father one without sin.

Envy

    He sits under a sixty watt bulb
    in his flaking efficiency apartment
    scanning the list of fortune's 500
    devouring society pages
    memorizing names he never knew
    creeping each day to his teller's cage
    miserable with what he has.
    A life of daytime dreaming
    and nighttime tossing on his cot,
    eating from tins of pork and beans
    when others dine on filet mignon
    with crystal goblets refilled
    of vintage Lafitte Rothschild.
    Picture books of Paris streets

and nights on silken sheets
at Bellagio in Las Vegas
a life gorged with wants
living other people's lives.
Green is his color, yet
he never walks a forest path,
strolls painting-filled museums
partaking the free and priceless.
Living in a cocoon of envy
playing Power Ball while
imagining satin and scepter.

Greed

Alone in her seven room apartment
littered with papers she cannot trash
counting again and yet again
her growing horde of stock certificates,
Hattie Green totaling today's wealth
leaving her home to pillage
returning to a bowl of soup and crackers.
She will die never having loved,
loathing even herself
tolerating the cats that share her hovel.
What tragic slap of chance
or times upon a sanding wheel
ground her mind so small
to only self-fulfilling hate.
She made herself a prison
who could have built Versailles.

Anger

What sport of faulty genes
create this rage bubbling
like tea in an unpoured pot,
a mind that only rests

in restless ticks of sleep.
Smashing his hand at the pane
he roils against himself and all
the others who are not him.
He dreams of suicide
or bursts of serial killing,
he must buy himself a rifle
willing murder indiscriminate,
his heroes, Hitler, Himmler
Caligula. Impotent
he rides his lumpy chair
awaiting awful inspiration.

Gluttony

Fat as a force fed hog
the glint of his diamond stickpin
echoing off his pinkie ring,
he settles in for dinner
oysters, beef, sturgeon, duck
coffee washing cherry pie.
He is the diamond Jim
incapable of fulfillment,
a charming peddler
wrapped in bespoke suits
silken shirts and cravats,
forever seeking happiness
at the end of a silver fork.
This is a lesser sin
harming no one but himself.

Sloth

Oblemov unable to rise
off his brocade sofa cushions,
heart beating slowly
waiting a sign to go up

to join the world, knowing
the flash will never come.
He has been gifted much,
his French crafted armoire
filled with unworn jackets
coats, trousers, astrakhans,
shoes of softest kid crafted
on lasts stored in chests,
powdered with thin dust veneer.
Servants bring dinner on trays
silver, his family crest beaten
in a pattern of sullen griffins,
this aged man, skin sagging, in diapers,
his wife, hump backed, speaking only
of her childhood, asking where is she
where have Mama, Papa gone.
Their apartment, life's last moment,
will be painted when they vacate.
Now dust encrusted chocolate
lying next the sink, her nightgown
crumpled on the sofa, last months papers
flung across the bedroom rug
trapped in the stasis.
Nonagenarians, they live on tv
saltines and cups of milk
dropping asleep, dropping awake.

Pride

Up here, look up here, my climb!
I see humans small as ants
there are forests, mountains, vast canyons
the race of giraffes and reboks.
I carry rubies, diamond tiaras,
tomes I have read, too difficult
for almost every other man.
Like Alexander, I have seen the Sphinx,

like Caesar crossed the Rubicon
walked the Stations of the Cross
strode the top of the Great Wall
in custom tuxedo, handmade shirt
sapphire cuff links, Rolex.
I gaze myself at the mirror
I cannot find the me that was.

The Wages of Fame

The hanging gardens of Babylon
are gone and its landscape architect
buried in a long forgotten tomb.
Men conceive of monuments
to escape the infinity of silence.
I remember Max, apartment builder,
the largest under one roof in the world.
He jumped out of the top floor window
when the bank foreclosed his dream.
Michelangelo lives in the Last Judgment
his body broken on the scaffold,
and who will read my scribbling.

The Nether World

Under the big tent,
spangled women flying
trapeze bars, wire dancing,
life is chance in the tiger cage
cats arrayed like dogs
instinctually waiting to pounce,
clowns rolling out the VW
and cotton candy whoops
elephants pirouetting,
obese ballerinas,
horses sprinkled silver
a riot of jogglers, dandies,
untouchable nomadic women,
an underworld of men.
While twenty yards past
the fattest woman on earth
sits like a spider,
the rubber man,
the donkey boy,
the dwarf, the ghoul,
the mellifluous ringmaster
master of magical rites
raking in the bucks.

Where Death is Terrified

There lies at the border
between earth and sun
a canyon filled with boiling acid
rushing, and the mountains
russet, trees bald but one
on one side of the divide
reaching across, a mother
seeking a fallen child.
Lemmings march the rim
and leap and float
escaping gravity and death.
This is the home of dragons
Yeti, the Jersey devil,
big foot, the one armed man
the place where myth is born
a place of screaming life
a place where death is terrified
to walk for fear that he
will lose himself in death.

We Retreat to Autobiography

As we crumble toward senility
former strength ebbing, memory
ever more selective, names
disappearing, faces fading
like ancient sepia prints,
memory of youthful sins,
bombard us obsessively
refusing erasure, iterating,
driving us to prayer.
Forgive our sins, that lay
like silt damming remembrance
of moments of nobility.
We retreat to autobiography
selectively excavating
the shards of honor
from the detritus of life.

Sheol

A minister, a Rabbi, a priest, an iman
met in the anti room of heaven
each expecting a festive feast
upon his entrance to eternal life.
As they waited, a man in work soiled jeans
entered, looked at each of them
and muttered "I believe in none of you"
and instantly was taken through the door
and ushered to the throne
by a quartet of angels singing
that the saint has finally come.

The All Mighty

At sixteen I was mad
for a uniform to trade
for the rags I wore
knowing everything
and all there was to learn
of my village and the world.
I joined our military
relearning the ways of men
learning their thoughts
learning even as a recruit,
after learning to wish to kill,
I learned that they would do
as I wished them.
They were weak and stupid
and I learned yes sir
to those of rank, those
like the kine of my tent.
Through years I fought wisely
drank and whored enough
since after losing me once
in acrid wine I woke
to Sunday sick, head in flames
and never lost my mind again.
I rose in rank
in wisdom, in rage
remembering to serve the mighty
pap and pandering and learned
that they were but my tent mates
older, richer, insecure with power.
I was wise and crouched
waiting for the fire of the mob
and when it came and I was ripe
with those I carefully had
primed to seize the throne.
I was the least, the voice

of those who grabbed the spoils
and sober when they, like swine
lapped the trough until my moment.
Now when I alone an emperor
for life – which will be long
for I will call sixteen year olds
from my army and neuter them
with wine and prostitutes
and those few sober of will
I immolate for treason.
I am the chess grand master
ruling the stupid barely fed
for as I was alone in barracks
I read and read of kings
and their usurpers, mobs
and revolution that comes
not from the rubble but those
well read and fed who move them.
Mein Kampf is my bible.
I build abstractions to hate
feast days to sate their bellies
random terror to dampen will.
I am both black and white
with many queens, no children
for I have read Oedipus.
Public auto-da-fé are good
parades of tanks are good
poison a cure for egoism.
I have a fenced villa
and wealth culled for rights
to mine my little earth
from nations that would tame me
and feed my nation's poor.
I am emperor for life
I am king of kings
I have risen to divinity
in twenty two years of war
I have become omnipotent.

The God of Cockroaches

I am a tiny god, a lover
of simplicity, cleanliness,
I need no liturgy, no service
no fasting, flagellation, sacrifice
in MY NAME. I need no temple
no statues, crowns, relics, saints.
My worshippers live in peace
living and dying modestly, quietly
scampering to evade monsters
without thought of retaliation
my subjects pray by living gently.

The God of Pygmies

On the first of each millennium,
the ancient gods gather to debate
the worthiness of human kind
to live or face annihilation.
Baal, Astarte, Jesus, Amon-Ra,
The Buddha, Allah, Yahweh, Zeus
Odin, tribal gods, forgotten gods
those who came to earth
and those proclaimed by surrogates
sit in muted convocation
pondering the worth of their creation.
They watch the bombs of sun multiply,
fruit of their making become extinct
their names excusing mutilation,
their words twisted into reasons
for man to kill and torture man.
Hera weeps they are but human
Mars laughs they are but toys
one moment before the final vote
for Armageddon is taken,
the god of pygmies speaks,
"they are so young, and few
so very few, have risen
to denounce the demagogues"
a few remembered, most
were killed. But the god of pygmies
speaks again, "it is true they are foolish
most are vile, most silent,
most wallow in the mud, pigs,
selfish caring only for the moment
but they are very young and some
so very few have hope and some
can see beyond themselves,
look on one tortured beyond Job

made mute, paralyzed, who
with it all still seeks out truth,
looks on the new-born Jeremiah
who calls on man to cease destructions."
The motion tabled until
the turning of the next millennium.

Why Not Shed Loneliness

Knowing that God is omniscient, omnipotent
and believing it are cast iron doors
separating my mind from my mind.
Why pluck a bigamous idolater
from Ur, a tongue tied orphan
from a harem, a mad woman
who believed she was a general
with whom to chat – why not
Caesar, Alexander, Mao, a Pope
to chew the fat discussing
wisdom, power, religion.
Why allow his son to feel forsaken
at the end. Why not shed loneliness,
enter an Irish pub, sip Guinness
enjoy some fun that He has made.

Denial

The death of the six million is
still denied
by those who will not notice
the near empty synagogues
Sabbath morning.
And where have the Gypsies
and those with misshaped bodies
gone?
Do those with numbers
tattooed on their arms
scream out in fitful sleep
and what of the now old men
who quietly returned post war
assuming new lives. Those men
who only followed orders.
Photos of shambling skeletons
were they also faked
to sell more papers?
The scrubbed concrete buildings,
the barracks still intact,
those wooden slat beds
the mounds of teeth and bones
were these imagined?

The End Game

The bomb ticks on a table.
I lie awake immobile, hearing
time dwindling, like a shrine
it stands blocking the window.
A man in the adjoining room waits
anticipating entrance to heaven.
I rise, invite him in, to play
a game of chess, we set the board
he opens poorly. King's pawn
I try a fool's mate, countered
we exchange men. Finally left
each with our solitary kings
endlessly marching the board
we will not declare a draw
moving square by square
until the universe finally ends.

Religion

And Thou Shalt Crawl

A snake, pipe cleaner thin
mottled sky blue, sea green
standing on its tail's tip
stretches upward toothless mute
beseeching Him to Pardon
the sin, not of deed, of temptation.
The sons of Eve walk, speak
while I crawl the earth
fertilizing the fields of sinners.
You have made me a pariah
I kill for food, to live
they kill for sport, some even
claim that right in Your name.
The Heavens split, a voice
a voice beyond Thunder
shouts IT IS DONE.

8TH DAY

On the eighth day of the creation of earth,
two angels were sent to watch what He had made.
Moneen, a strict and righteous judge,
Brindeen called Loki by generations of men,
reporting the death of Abel. God said
return and watch but do not interfere.
I have given all my creatures minds,
capacity to learn, we must see
what they make of all I've given them.
In time one creature learned arrogance
and made of itself saints and monsters.
The angels suggested we must slay them,
but the Lord said we shall wait
they may grow wise or else
they may, in time, destroy themselves.

The Exit from Eden

Blazing swords of Seraphin
rushing toward him, Adam
imbued with knowing evil
and knowing good, ran
from God in fear from Eden.
Eve, alone, slunk from the oasis
enceinte of the serpent's seed,
seeking her significant other
fearing the lightning flash of death
and the reappearance of Lilith.
They finally met, embraced
talking through days and nights
for there was no one else
to assuage the loneliness
of nothing, but to forage food
after the euphoria of naming.
Two strangers traumatized,
alone to rear their issue.
What dysfunction gendered murder
recrimination bred a race
eschewing Eden's lure
eschewing peace for war eternal
while the Seraphin await return.

And Where is the God of the Ram

While Abraham climbed Ararat
Isaac bearing fire wood
Sarah lay weeping
cursing his mad god,
kidnapper of her joy
who gives but takes
ounce for ounce.
Vowing she will never
speak to her husband
who has reached insanity,
hearing a voice no other
hears, following the chimera
he calls Adonai, monster
who would kill her son
without discussion.
She hates him as no wife
before loathed her spouse
and prays to god
to make him sane again.

God the Idol

Squatting, arms thrust forward
its back straight. An emerald,
big as a human fist, sunk
above its aquiline nose,
one eye to avoid equivocation,
it stands in the high hut's center.
Supplicants circle it begging.
Celebrants giving thanks,
all blessings from this megalith,
this thing in the image of man
legend says appeared one morning
full grown in the hut of a mystic
who then lived tending its needs,
interpreting its meanings,
gathering its offerings.
The tribe named itself
sons of the green stone
and lived with their otherness
knowing they possessed divinity

Ancient Ghettos

A people forced to introspections
walls shut tightly to restrain
them from infecting those
illiterate folk filled with lore
of blood rites, of secret cabals,
of plots to rule the earth.
From squalid hovels,
claustrophobic ghettos
Yeshivahs where every sentence
is parsed for subtleties
for meaning within meaning.
Powerless, imagining a Golem
to defend their very lives
to preserve a nation of martyrs.
There was no Golem
when they were packed in boxcars
scholars become slaves,
corpses, or harvesters of bones.
The remnant finally
become a land of Golems.

The Real and Truly God

Perhaps the real and truly god
is neither Yahweh, Jesu
Allah nor Mahmed
but Loki lying in dark alleys
to leap out in jester's cap
bells and rabbits appearing
from empty air. A god
who chuckles, a god
who saws the earth in half.

Perhaps there is no dour judge
nor one who pardons solemnly
but a jaunty boulevardier
plucking aces from the sky
laughing at man's inanities
punishing saints and canonizing
idiots. Believing God is good
and evil an unexplainable
aberration -- Believing omnipotence
defies logic. We can choose
the laughing trickster. Or nothing.

Dec. 28, 2008

Mocking the atrocities of man
Gaia wafted perfumed air
and breezes tinged with warmth
while children of the ancient tribes
of Jacob and of Esau die
ignoring their biblical reconciliation.
Are we molded by our planet's
tectonic plates, tsunamis,
hurricanes dicing the works of man?
This day lulls me calm.
I would thrust my arms
to heaven, parting the waters
holding back the tides.
The breezes gust, dancing trees,
fallen leaves blown off bushes.
My arms are impotent
Gaia will not be quiet.

CHRISTMAS

Trees sprout stars, ornaments
gilt and silver, blinking lights.
Tables spread with ham, yams
the season of snow flakes.
Santas begging for the poor.
Children anticipating gifts
to toy with and fast forget.
A time to say we love all men
while murder takes no holiday.
Some manic some depressed
dour shopkeeps hope to smile
a time of somber services
a child's birth celebrated.

All Hallows Eve

Spirits not only rise
from ill made crypts on Hallows Eve
but flit across the land
like slowly circling hawks
unquieting human sleep
to whisper ancient memories
to resurrect forgotten instincts
when we would run the other race
walked tree crammed hills and sing
of randy love and sing of buttons.
Those witches with their apple breasts
and lips and mandolins
torment me in those moments
of sentient sleep when minds
fade to grey and dance in scarlet
when cicadas dance to mate
when shadows cross the moon
the dead rise daily to torment
the aged whispering lullabies
of cradles and of time to sleep.

The Second Coming

At the end of the world
inherited by the meek
waited, hushed in clouds
for the second coming.
Filled of an inner shining
he came, hands raised
to bless the earth
his voice soft in prayer
he came with redemption
a missionary from God
to end sin, decree peace
announce the second Eden.
He found that man was gone
and he was preaching
to the roaches and algae.

The Horsemen

Lank centaurs streaking the very
continent, Battery to Golden Gate Park
famine, disease, poverty, death
gifts they bring with crackling skies,
California chateaus toppling down hill
the bayou reclaiming its city
coffins rising with the flood
bearing bones for orphaned dogs.
A second sun appears, the moon dies,
Old Nick cackles in his furnished cave
split level all modern conveniences
hot and cold harlots, pigeon shoots
waterboarding games for fun
and funny games for real.
This is the moment of salvation
but there is no savior
false messiahs bearing placards
my end is near. You are lost.
Truth on bumper stickers,
office seekers screaming invective,
bigotry for profit and fame,
sages spewing nonsense.
All times are times of trouble
and the horsemen ride unchallenged.

The Inferno

Finegan tumbled down stairs
his wake a midnight dream.
Dante's descent to hell
without a guide, without
Paula and Francesca embracing
floating out of time in space,
Hitler, Tojo, Mussolini embracing
eternally, with acid coated skins.
Sadam and Idi Amin
wondering at the power of power.
Those who seek dominion
over those they see as lesser things
have a special niche with Satan,
the judge of those who walk the earth.
When is the millennium of peace?
When will Charon's craft be moored?

I Sense a Second Universe

The world appears within my mind
a cloud of ash expanding,
a bit of leaf pulverized
between my thumb and second finger,
people small as ants and giants
tall as Everest tramp behind sight
in the crevice behind my retina.
I sense a second universe
where the detritus of this world
gathers lustful and reborn,
as lint imbued with life
flies the sunbeam dancing
as it parachutes to floor.
My mind cluttered with mysteries
so convoluted I cannot solve
the crossword or mesh the pieces
of the black and grey jigsaw.
The answer on a Ouija Board
the pointer riding the surface
like a black ant gliding
stopping, forward, side, back
and each time spelling only yes

The Agony of Earth

Unless the agony of earth is but a test
why not flood, comet or fire?
Why spare Noah when saints are few
and lust, a nameless creature
lumbering all foul down hill,
rules the world. An immigrant
building a stake penny by penny
working three jobs, buys a store
is killed over thirty dollars in the till
by an addict who could not add to thirty.
We will have spent more on his death
than ever spent to give him a life
where his only asset was his gun,
sold to him by a man in a shop
more costly than the victim's store.

Nightmare

A man of moon round face
and skin grey as a fox
with fangs, visage of Satan,
hangs above my bed, smiling
teeth green and melting
a trumpet screams me awake
the ceiling bursts open
a universe of stars rush down.
I am awake in sweat and fear,
this is the final judgment.
I am discovered wanting

The Penitent

In a desert cabin, mad
with visions of god's heaven,
his mind drifting drifting
on the oceans of space
like leaves in the currents
of earth, clasped hands prays.
He has renounced humanity
abandoned all earthly creatures
giving himself to himself
visioning hell a mountain
spewing boiling lava on those
embedded in rock below.
So he plots to save himself
while God shrugs and lists him doomed

The Seer

The seer on the mountain
enveloped in eider down
wrapt in regret
peruses the stars
mumbling earthly lore
seeking the final vision.
He squats alone.
The visitor will appear
clanging cymbals
bearing gifts of wafers
sitting silently
as the moon fades to light

The Universe

This thing we call our universe
is but a statue, a decoration,
in the living room of God.
Of malleable substance
part expanding, part collapsing,
it is an ever changing work
He fashioned and peruses
In times of solitude and leisure,
the stars, the planets are the atoms
of His latest masterwork,
few are populated by microscopic things
dusted off when they cease to amuse
or let evolve for Him to contemplate
the unexpected possibilities.
He smiles at times when some
tiny constructs, together or alone,
pray to Him, believing
they would be uninvited guests
in his ephemeral mansion
as if it were not enough that
He allowed them to become
and does not crush and refashion
this abstract work formed by his hands.
Yes, He can shrink himself
and has become a swan, a flame,
a bit of entertainment in a solitary,
sometimes boring, endless life.
He sometimes ponders who fashioned Him
and sometimes prays to that unknown
and wonders if He too will be swept away
and wonders if He is awfully alone.

The Highest Court

The river rides the valley
down crags, down mottled patches
of grass, briers and marigold,
it is a twisted garden hose
where tadpoles flit with carp
and nymphs and satyrs dance
on moonless starless nights.
This river is the feeder stream
where Charon sailed his resumé,
black bottled lowland scotch
and tins of cookies for his would be boss.
That was an interview of life and death
winner take all and Charon won
the oar, the boat, the fiercest dog
eternal occupation, eternal pet.
Charon is the final court with
power to pardon, turn spirits back
denying passage, offering redemption
at the river's terminus, the site
where the river feeds the river Styx.

The Last Judgment

On the last day
the last figure complete,
Michaelangelo hobbled down
his scaffold, aching
maddened by the wonder
the universe of paint
the empty skin, dropped
like trash to the river.
He contemplated in pain
his only final masterpiece
collected his last wages
and drank away the night

Yom Kippur

This is a day of autumn chill
of dreaded possibilities
the remnant of the sons of Avram
gather unfed attaining rapture
intoning at the setting of the sun
god is one, the eternal one is one.
They summon Him to judge
to pardon all communal sins
to forget, forgive their own
allowing them another summer.
This day begins at night
Kol Nidre the tune a dirge
remembering Torquemada
the scourge, a hundred Hamans
hating them, the others,
huddling in ghettos in camps
watching their mothers burn
the wisps of human smoke.
Those now leeching uranium
envisioning a final solution
an epic auto de fé for those
who pray a world of peace.

A Prayer

I. Dawn

First light infuses darkened spruce
with patches of grey, a blanket
layers thick and dappled, sunlight
daubed on trunks past branches.
I slept fitfully and rose and read
and watched the daily miracle
thanking the master builder that
I had been allowed another day

II. Day

Robots clump metal to metal
a single part repetitively.
I muse out the garage
down driveway, turn
up the hill, turn, turn
and turn, park and enter,
routine honed through decades
messages, emails, faxes
piled to scan and ponder.
I am paid for what I think
I know, I draft and talk
negotiate and in seldom moments
contemplate, spew advice, ideas
like papers blown down Broad Street.
I am like a spider waiting flies
lunching at my table by the phone
companion to a Dictaphone
and sometimes march to court
like Shane with briefs for guns
and words for ammunition.

I then retrace my drive
to home, to peace, to read
of other lives and times
to watch TV stupidity
at news that is not news
but other people's angst.

III. Dusk

Yellow shard like collage
pasted behind cloud wisps
my pulse slows, we will eat
describing the daytime day
and if we fail to bicker
turn our minds to off
await the possibility of sleep.

IV. Night

I cannot sleep regurgitating
problems of the afternoon
scribbling notes, to dos
and not dos
I cannot build a car
plant food or plan a home.
I roll from side to side
pray for sleep to numb
my mind that never sleeps.

Aging

The Round of Day

Awakening from a muddled dream
of prayer mumbled in an alien church,
flying through rainbow clouds
naming a child we never had.
Addled eyes glued, unsure
whether to rise or lie abed
interpreting those dreams or
plotting how to use the day,
a gift diminishing each hour.
I leap out, shower, shave
daub ointment to salve
the pain of aging skin
ingesting pills to staunch
the inexorable tide of time
and start the daily round
of email, fax and telephone,
anticipate an evening dose
of scotch carefully distilled
by brewers I will never meet
so days melt into days
until I finally drift asleep

The Retirement House

Gathering to be ushered to dinner
restless on walkers or squat
in motorized wheelchairs, the lucky
on canes or *mirabile dictu*
somewhat erect, somewhat bent
some speak haltingly, some mute.
They have passed fear of death
scanning the menu, food their last
taste of sensuality.
They speak of grandchildren,
children, forgetting names, aliens
in different cities, states
universes, never the departed
only apartments vacant
wondering who will fill them.
This is the grave's anteroom
this is hell's doorway
the home of the fortunate.

Old Age

Skin miraculously heals itself
while mind and bones whither,
memory retreats to the edge of age
feet walking brush the floor,
a limp replaces steady strides.
They sit in anterooms of hell
walkers shoved in dining nooks
wheelchairs replacing stately chairs.
They still can eat and stare
Companions, mainly black, tenderly
wiping spittle from their lips.
They speak little of the dead
and less of world events
for they have left the world.
Their children dutifully visit
once a week chattering inanities
to fill the time until they leave.
A few grandchildren race the halls
oblivious to time and place.

Each Same Day Disappears

Grasping for words
as she grasps her walker
each same day disappears
at sleep at night.
Names are an etch a sketch
erased in a moment
replaced by the sense
that they are gone.
Those people say
they are her children
she accepts them
as if they are
she wheels the corridors
groping a name, hers
her childhood was yesterday.
Terrified of change
afraid of places
beyond the building
where she is free
existing as she must
by rote, by instinct
her age has disappeared
into childhood memory,
at dinner with her sisters
father at the head, mouth set
a mighty wall of rectitude
mother kindly ordering the maid
to serve the entrée.
Her marriage sixty eight years ago
has not yet happened, her groom
snapshots jumbled in time
cinema verte edited by Joyce.
One day she will forget to breathe
and in that moment will she
see it all flash within her mind.

Senility is Heaven's Anteroom

Proudly rising to stride her room,
when she had not walked in years,
she fell. She will not remember
the origin of the purple bruise
nor the moment when she stood again.
Senility is heaven's anteroom.
Nurtured by long dead parents,
playing with sisters, brothers,
childhood's friends, the living
have disappeared, shut from memory.
The aged woman of the mirror is gone
the strangers who tend her are nice
or cause her fear, she is calm
or trembling in panic. Each day
rising in a place she's never been
she returns to her first home
as she nears the final mystery.

Birthday Party

Sun glows the room
a rose on every table
smooth gliding coasters
on every plush chair.
Women with their daughters,
sons-in-law, sit rigid
remembering school day friends,
buffet spread with salad
fruit, scrambled eggs
cheese, bacon, herring
smoked salmon, muffins
final pleasure of the aged.
The daughters load plates
to assuage weeks apart,
for trips are very far.
Visits wake memories of
when they were tended.
Half sentences dangle
their beginning forgotten.
Stories told, retold, retold,
until the daughter, mouth clenched
mutters yes we heard it
and trembles at the vision
of herself...her daughter
sitting silent, crumbs
sprinkling her blouse.

The Past Reappears

Living solely in the present
memory filtered between beginnings
and this moment of awakening,
she is an aged child,
parents long dead reborn
in the day's forgotten past.
New found anger at her mind
as it gradually disappears,
each day becoming Saturday,
yesterday and tomorrow faded
unsure of place and time.
This is the fate of women
finally alone, finally living
in rooms, walls contracting,
grasping for words, sentences
unable to order lunch
having what her table mate has
and, at last, forgetting to awake.

In the Nursing Home

Arrayed and silent as the monoliths
of Stonehenge, the wrinkled shrunken women
fixed in wheelchairs face a TV screen
asleep or await their long dead parents'
dinner invitation. The home is clean
scrubbed of the smell of ancient flesh.
Young women, underpaid, wheel them
to and from the toilet, to bed,
to lunch, where they unspeaking eat
water dribbling down their chins
amid a klatch of pills and pap.
Death is unacknowledged here.
Families notified, meet in other homes
to mourn the long dead mother
aunt or cousin rarely seen
while left to the care of strangers

A Scrap of Paper

Wedged in a fetal crouch
atremble from cold and Thunderbird,
a sheet thin blanket dotted with holes
like paper punched by a child
covers his soiled and staring body.
The burghers speed-walk past him
deliberately eyeing the street
rejecting that this could be them.
The press reports the doing, the buying
of the latest billionaire but
neglects the coterie of new made paupers.
A woman, robbed of memory by dementia,
is shipped to a paupers facility
when her funds, gathered by scrimping
a lifetime have trickled away
month by month to the nursing home,
a link in a publically owned chain
controlled by a face in newsprint.
The street person will die, perhaps
a sister unseen for decades
will recognize him, the paper
will report his passing on page one —
Harvard grad, professor of English,
disappeared twelve years ago
after his divorce, his firing
the townsfolk will glance the headline
and turn quickly to the sports page.

Immortality

We sketch our lives in sand
expunged each night in tides
that crawl the beach
erasing the day's heroics.
A pebble hurled lakewise
remembered ripples disappear.
A great man dies,
the earth spins, unmoved.
We still can read his words
remembering his face
in fading photographs.
All seek immortality
an oasis carved from the earth,
but the winds
whirling cover the grave.

Funding university structures
we seek immortality
until the wreckers ball
or storm eradicate them.
Whatever, lives fade
by the fourth generation,
a name only on family trees
the struggles finally lost.

The Reaper

At a dash or saunter
with dagger or gentle touch
he is pictured a skeleton
bearing a silver scythe
epitome of evil even
by those who picture heaven
iteration of Eden or
country club or orgy.
But he is elegant, wise
bespoke suits from
Savile Row, shoes
of softest kid
linen shirts from Hong Kong
ties spun silk from Paris.
He will finally seduce
each woman, share cocktails
with every man on earth.
He is the physician
of the final consult
he is our last friend
he is neither proud nor humble
holding all knowledge
his appointment book is full
at times to overflowing
he makes his daily rounds
without mistake or pity.

A Funeral

An old man will be buried today
ashes from a voluntary *auto da fé*
swept into his urn, placed in dirt.
Children will surround the plot
grandchildren, a few who
served on boards with him.
He wanted no legate of god
no kaddish – someone will speak
neglecting to mention the years
he sat, wheelchair bound,
almost mute, incontinent
praying silently for death
the final nurse, to find him.
He will be spoken of discreetly
and they will walk away
anticipating their inheritance.

War and Destruction

The Second Sodom

On the eighth day, the One
summoned two of his advisors
Madeem, the judicious, the wise,
the dour who would be named
with many names as Jove, Elija,
and Ladeem, the laughing one
called, in later times, Loki
Jupiter, Leprechaun, His favorite.
"Go to the little toy I made,
the ball I tossed to the firmament,
and see if it is worthy to be saved."
They saw the great lumbering creatures
arisen from the waters
existing solely to eat, to survive.
Madeem said they were worthless,
Ladeem said they were amusing
but unworthy of Your greatness,
and so He wiped the ball clean
and in the evening of the eighth day
made little things with minds
able to understand their fate.
Again Madeem and Ladeem were sent
Madeem said these little things
are unworthy, true they pray
but use Your name to prey prey prey
on their own kind, their greed unbounded
they foul your ball, terrorize
their lesser kin. Ladeem said but
a few of them are wise, some
tend their sick, some seek You
truly, some tend their flocks
wisely, a few are worthy.

The One thought deeply. Although
the scales bent toward destruction,
He pondered while the ball spun
and finally proclaimed "I will wait
to see if they destroy themselves."

Spins the Bottle

The celluloid ball is flipped to serve
and as the paddle strikes it
dissolves to plastic powder ash
wafting from a campfire in Maine.
The dank and spongy green of earth
in a winter mist of rain
odor of peat and rotting apples.
The silence of a robin grazing,
a rabbit chased by a poodle
flies to pine's top branch
and the poodle trots to its stylist.
A clip and a pedicure
and its off to romp through leaves.
Flecks of yellow fill interstices
of the branches of spruce.
The sun just risen borne
by boat obliterating dusk,
while a tiger runs the veldt.
A child is born to rags.
His mother, in terror, tucks him
neatly in a bassinet
and gently leaves him at a stable
where suckled by dappled mares
he will grow to found New Rome.
The pebble spins the universe
of mystical imaginings and dung.
A bottle spins selecting she
to kiss the wounded hero.
The king of hearts takes the throne
while groundlings watch his installation.
The bishop, censor and wafer
moves from his room and board
intoning pig latin earbyhay
essblayotectpray fenday.

Citizens rush the palace
a mob sprinkling carrots
until a smiling moon
decrees the lunatics shall rule.

Never Again

If all those killed
in the human abattoir
and the children never born arose,
the weight of their tears
would hurl this world past Mars.
We have finally made ourselves a land
from the bones of Buchenwald
where we can own a tractor
direct traffic, teach and trade
and build ourselves an army.
We have taken brittle sand
and from it moulded forests,
olive groves, orchards, farms,
turned victims from the Steppes,
the Nile, the fertile crescent,
our Ethiopian cousins
and made them scholar-soldiers.
Never again will Cossacks,
Crusaders, inquisitors
use us as they slaughter pigs.
Never again will we be driven
to killing fields, crematoria,
concrete showers of gas.
This people of Freud, Marx
Spinoza, Rashi, the Rambam,
this people of Nobel laureates
fishermen, even Jesus Christ
whose words and death were
turned to stones to strike us,
never again will we
walk terrified to slaughter.

Birth of a Nation

Spawned from the blood
and tattooed arms of
thousands of the millions dead
declaring nationhood waiting
a holocaust of armour
prepared with bullets smuggled
in cigarette packs, rifles
bought in back alley meetings
with dollars gathered clandestinely
from hotel owners, pharmacists
from doctors, lawyers, CPA's
giving for the dream, the prayer
next year in Jerusalem
giving for a nation in utero
giving to Irgun terrorists
against his majesty's empire.
Eddie, the haberdasher, wheedling
recognition from his old friend
who loved him, not the people
who would honor Balfour's promise
as Balfour's kin withdrew
bequeathing guns, tanks
to those who would drive
the survivors, the remnant
into the sea. The planes
stopping only to refuel
wheeled from front to front
the few becoming a fleet.
The army of scholars, farmers, doctors
fighting for their children's lives.
Never again, never again.
They made a nation on sand
land wasted for millennia
a land where milk and honey

lay waiting rebirth
Herzel's dream realized.
Preserving the Mosques, churches
sacred places of others
healing their wounded enemies
in hospitals built by women
with scrimped household dollars.
Gathering the despised
from every continent.
A nation born of ashes
from crematoria, killing fields.
A nation of the chosen,
chosen for death. Oh god mourn
the sacrificial lambs
the scapegoats of the earth.

In the Shadow of Horror

(NY Times 9/19/07)

After eight hours of killing
it was good to sun oneself
on beach chairs and joke
with pretty frauleins.
Efficient extermination is hard
accepting men as cattle
at Buchenwald , accepting Fuhrer
as savior, omniscient god
and then to sing some lieder
play with puppies, eat heartily
and sleep without dreams of death.

The Game

I rolled the lead tank
beside a twig, camouflaged it
under a leaf and waited
until the two truck convoy
rode past and yelled boom boom,
and my lead soldiers
attacked the marksmen in the truck
and both of us yelled bang bang,
and some fell over but we
didn't know what death was.
When I was older they shaved
my head, handed me a rifle
and told me learn to kill.
Plunged to the bottom of my mind
peeled potatoes, slept on garbage
march hour on hour until
I thought only of my feet
and the pack and the M-1.
I was driven so beyond sleep
I might have followed orders
but I never had the opportunity
and hope I wouldn't have followed
for I was no longer a child.

On Patrol

A sheath of bravado,
swaggering, as eyes pendulum,
seeking the site from which
death may flash, no skeleton
cloaked in black, a child
a girl, a birthday boy.
These khaki suited children,
beer or smack to mask night,
an endless mission
in a foreign place,
the smell of hate
at every rutted street.
They have been sent
by stolid dour men
who come to say they've been
and leave knowing nothing
while they, abandoned
left to kill, to die,
as names upon a wall.
We walk the rows at Normandy
the forests of Bastogne
the rolling hills at Shiloh
the farms at Gettysburg
to see to weep aloud
to mourn the living
recite the Kaddish
and try to sublimate
the fear of death
in unpronounceable villages.

In Boot Camp Waiting

The soldiers massed along the ridge
rifles strapped across their backs
backpacks crammed with military gear
and at the signal raced down,
forded the river, boots sopping,
the wind like shrapnel tearing cheeks,
a ten mile trot around the town
and back to camp to smoke and sleep.
Next day and next until their minds
are ground to sand, their legs
taut as cast iron, arms prepared
to follow any order, ready to kill
whatever enemy their elders picked.
Ancient men with ancient minds
alighting from chauffeured limousines
to plan campaigns they never saw
unable to see past devastation,
reveling in power they imagined,
wisdom they professed, blind
to what they will have done.

After the Kill

The syrupy aroma of blood
noxious odor of offal
blend where cows are sliced
to slabs served rare
in faux Tudor rooms
to groups of puffy men.
Out after daylong negotiations
for scotch, cigars and meat,
trading superficial tales
jokes botched by amateurs.
Their wives, Penelopes, home
cooking for the children
while they, brash heroes,
boast, voices losing modulation
as the whiskey reaches blood.

The Beachhead

Rafts, ships sunk by cannonade
emptied oil drums are the breakwater,
a calm water, washing shell pocked sand
under hills where bunkers lay
awaiting cargo off the landing boats,
emerging like Pickett's men to death
to fill the future cemeteries,
symmetrical wedding white rows
of stones, a name, dates, a cross,
a star, a scimitar, a life compressed
another ground hallowed by blood
another tract where only grass will grow.
Amid this midnight silence
a whisper of the planes, the bombs
grenades, rifles recoil seventy years
echoing across the concrete redoubts.
Old men return on canes, walkers
in wheelchairs to give homage
to pray for those who barely lived.

July 4, 2007-1776

Neither stars nor moon nor
rockets blasting mark the day,
but only the rare firefly
when a huddle of men broiling
in miasmic heat of the city
proclaimed the primacy of man
over the institutions they make.
Risking the gallows for posterity
risking fortunes amassed honorably,
for a vision of untrained farmers
challenging a disciplined army.
But dreamers trump regiments
in defense of sacred honor.
On that day in that place
they inscribed their names
to paper that in other days
in other times meant death.
The border between treason
and patriotism is electrode thin.
At Trenton, Valley Forge
their children froze and died
for grandchildren and those
in distant lands unborn,
to risk their lives escaping
to el dorado, streets of gold
whose children could read
the words they endorsed
and fight their fight for freedom.

Real Politik

We now chat in non-rooms
text across the continents
teleconference with dozens of
faces, words enscreened
ravage and kill with buttons
victims never seen by men
severed arms depicted on a box.
We have made a world of hell
creating efficiency, losing humanity.

Where Mad Men Rule

The world is safe again
to play at games and contemplate
the pink and mauve of setting suns,
while children die in Africa
while nucleonic waste dumps stand,
while guns are sold in alleyways
like crack cocaine and sweaty sex,
while television reeks from candidates
spouting semi-truths to woo
a semi-literate populace to vote
against the other. This world
has always cultivated strange fruit
and pills to cure invented illness.
This world of poverty and excess
this unstable world our only home
where mad men rule and lemmings
have not yet learned to swim.

JIHAD

Preserving the power of death,
of terror, these pinched men
jeered at us children, shunned
as uncoordinated at soccer,
require obedience from women
flail at non-existent enemies,
spend their nation's wealth
building the bomb to obliterate earth.
They speak as though god-allah
was their ventriloquist.
We need a new bedlam
for those who order torture
as though it were a biscuit.
Now thousands march the streets.
How few men such as they
die in peace in quilted beds?
Do they wake to nightmare
visions of Mussolini
hanging head down on a post,
Hitler in his suicidal bunker,
Sadaam hanged, Stalin poisoned,
Caesar stabbed, Alexander
slain by syphilis. These men
have their little lives
of power, time of revenge.
Will they, Napoleon, Baby Doc, Il Duce
live at last in exile or
will their heads be stuck on pikes?
We have spawned them
in acquiescence and fear.
They are prestidigitators
pointing toward the others
Roma, Jews, homosexuals
infidels, and we hand them

our children to march as martinets
to strap bombs on their bellies
to train to kill and to die
so they can smile in luxury.
Do those few ever weep?
Do they scream asleep
for the horror that they reap?

HER COUCH OF SILENCE

I. Morning

The couch of silence is a pit of frigid dreams,
restless longing, leisurely ennui
and silent the fleshy woman approaches
her tomb of sighs and sits in flowered gown,
noontime slippers, silken negligee
with husband at his desk of commerce,
children at their ludicrous desks of knowledge
maid busily cleaning the glass partitions
cook at her aluminum skillet
all in its place and God in his heaven.

Engine chinook and screel banged in the morning wake
of headache, yawns and tossing, while the creature of the other bed
awoke and scratched and groped before the bathroom mirror,
the lady of the room crunched herself together under sheet
eyes closed so to abnegate the light, Day,
and husband waddled to his restaurant cup of coffee

and off to work, while his wife crept, hair unkempt,
into the littered bedroom to open the school day,
and padded down to cook the eggs and toast
in print-faded bathrobe cord frayed, unmade face, drooped eyes
a sight to frighten even those that sat, to school.

And then the maid and cook uneasily came through back doors
and silently started dusting and cooking the nighttime meal
while mistress, bathrobe daintily open to the knees, thought on the day
entombment of her friend, unseen three years,
enduring the hypocritic eulogy
a pilgrimage to that brown plot, the last home
and thinks, "it might be me, this could be me,
how soon, how many younger friends are gone?"
While clinging to the spider thread of life

the bloated woman rolls stomachward,
flips the television switch already set
to Mrs. Junovenovulcan's Troubles
and to the sugary voices of the world
sleeps.

II. The Well of Her Dream

Water is the well of her dream
softly hissing smoke
lava-filled water. The serpent
slithers through the slime caked bottom,
only water turbulent,
rushing in thousand high breakers,
and in small pools the hushed sound
cona misha seya dunna weash.

The fury of one finned giant
snapping at the other's neck
huge bubbles pop from the breeding sea.
A cloud, impenetrable, opaque,
covers the waves from the possible moon,
and the weaker reptile dies ungroaning.

Water is violent, jagged, pitted
in its depths--steam leaping,
geysers spurting into the calmer strata,
bodies intertwining
one into the other in the horrid conflict
scurrying to survive,
sea grey and foam whipped.
And in its black core
the struggle of creation and procreation,
for food, for rest, in a restless beginning.

Beneath the bottom
a volcano in eruptive tumescence
presaging land,
an invisible creature, plant-beast
lives and multiplies in the midst of the deep.

I was young and slim
no beauty, but
my stomach flat
my breasts firm
like bosc pears
and I had ripened
with a smile
and eyes of sunlight.
The photo he took
I glance at
buried in my sweater drawer.
When I've looked at me
too long, in my mirror
and seek the me I was.
He taught history,
philosophy, injected
Vico, Toynbee to my mind.
He had a Van Dyke beard
that tickled my forehead
and I was so in love
and so in lust.
He talked of worlds gone
in class and in
his bedroom
and I, trembling,
or so it now seems,
absorbed all of him.
Oh I had had
my little flings
my backseat disappointments
nocturns on the sofa

but this was passion
I'd read about
in novels set in France,
Venice, or Maracaibo.
In his elegant apartment
crammed with books
and prints depicting ruins,
the world that was,
and one Picasso etching
a few lines only,
a man, bullheaded,
clasping a startled girl,
and I was so in love
that year, and so alone,
when after graduation
he wrote to me from Rome
nothing that could be used
in an investigation
a short note, sans adjectives,
a letter of dismissal.
I tore it and burned it
and watched the ashes
singe in my toilet
curl black at the edges
fold and quickly melt.
I didn't cry
I was so damn mad
until I thought and thought
and knew, finally,
I had used him just as I
was his that year's distraction.
And he, like Dedalus,
trapped in the maze
but not to soar
while I would marry
and I did.
I saw his obit in the Times

and it was short
his few books his only progeny.
I imagined him old, bald,
creaking on his cane
and did he ever think on me
as I have dwelt on him.

The print encased woman groans and turns
asleep hearing the pitchman's staccato voice
like a cracked record spinning. Sweating
she tosses on her down cushions
kimono awry, damp,
in the haze of kitchen smells.

III. The Moment Before Noon

Once the lovely Narador
walked the reed encrusted shore
(drums call the men to war)
weary she lay and slept
the crocodile saw and gently took her
thus was born a son our father
(chants drive the men to war).

There was a time when the waters,
angered, rose filling the land
before the days of Narador
and now the stream is dying
and we must go far, seeking game
by the great waterfall.
Pig, leopard, antelope we may kill
but the crocodile we adore.
for therein lies the lives of all
(dance leads the men to war).

My son you were a boy
soon a man (oh, my child,
my child) walk not in fear
be brave (my baby)
tomorrow you will bear arms
and sit at the council
(and be gone, oh my little child).

Trembling he nears the cave of mystery
rock slivers pierce his feet, no pain
only the wonder of coming manhood.
As a child, yesterday, he heard
of Wonduga, the demon who swallows
in one gulp those who come to him.
He enters the monster's cave
sees the dead, guts spewed.
Tiptoeing over their bodies
he walks trembling in purple shadow
toward the old man seated deep in darkness.
With a shout the dead rise
rushing from the sacred place.
After cut of circumcision,
bleeding, he learns of tribe
the way of life, "thou must
at war smear thyself
with serpent blood;
thou must, when taking a mate,
place her on the great stone;
thou must not, when she is huge,
eat fruit fallen to earth."
He hides
until healed
and is returned to home
and weeping mother.

In council the master sits silent
the elders squatting below him

for it is the season of migration
and the time of tale-telling.
Our fathers found stone, to kill,
fire to warm and cook,
stalks and berries to eat
and the land, our land
to hold in war.

Slowly the tribe moves north,
seeking game, finding a fertile valley
rests, plants grain and later
hunters too till the soil
the master becomes the leader of men.

This drought blisters tongues
crops shrink, all weep for rain
lest they die.
The wizard
leads out a black man,
fettered, from the peaked hut
while the men of the tribe
squat in rows, goose-down
fixed to their bodies with blood.
Chanting from dawn for clouds,
the black clouds that bear rain.
At frigid night
the man is brought
before the silent council
then the dirge again
"bring rain, let clouds form
let clouds part, bring rain
bring rain, let clouds form
let clouds part, bring rain"
face down, is laid
across two black rocks
before the assembly, the wizard
hunched over his head

"bring rain, let clouds form
let clouds part, bring rain
bring rain, let clouds form...."
Knife raised sternum pierced
shriek stifled in chanting.

In spring they sow,
dance in lusting leaps,
they search, at times, for game
for water, to mate
to bear children to suck the breast.
And when their world is quiet
They work clay, painting crocodiles
upon their eating bowls.

IV. Early Afternoon

Awake, she walks the half-flight of stairs,
languidly dressing, dreading afternoon
then down, instructions to the cook and maid,
then out along the stone steps by the rhododendron
and her day's first glance at the ascending sun.
The car percolates in the garage then slowly out the drive
along the line of tree shaded suburban homes
alike but their colors. Traffic compresses
at every stop-light and she is glad for each delay.
Past the tailored lawns of quarter acre plots
past Wright's prayer house that leaks
on the pates of the faithful, a symbol
of God as giver of rain, or man
as sloppy artisan. Past the plaza
where she and her friend ate often,
their last meal together when they laughed
and dreamt about the future
and wondered the what ifs

that only old friends can exchange.
Then the instantly changing terrain
to city, an oasis becoming a desert,
down the long straight street
past the shuttered Burger King
past the homes, shells
like London in forty-four
in trembling and fear she pops the door locks
stares at the whores by the abandoned factory
past the great medical center
named for the protagonist of the bomb
past oriental groceries, chicken and rib shacks
under the trestle and along
the border of the university
a banner extolling the virtues
of its football team
glancing at the other cars, pedestrians
and upward to Billy Penn
dressed in Quaker black
one hand raised, the other
at his lower parts
past shops, apartment buildings,
offices and office buildings
into town and garages
to lunch alone.
Standing at Peter and Paul
the bare chested bearers of loaves
framed in glass and Georgian stone
she stares at fountains,
pennants, down the great boulevard
to the repository of armor, plates
and cracked glass.
She crosses to the restaurant
orders, eats without tasting
and out and driving, driving.
Finally she sees the funeral home, white marble,
gaudy in affected Doric. She parks the car

and walks slowly down the street, then into the chapel
clasps hands with her few acquaintances there
thinking, "who will be next in the silent tomb?"
At last she creeps ahead to view the woman lying beyond sleep,
pauses her instant and rushes away to sit
thinks of her children, her husband and the good days
while the reverend drones on in prayer, in eulogy.
We would go to the Crystal Tea Room
for lunch and chat
about our high school classmates
particularly those
who'd snubbed us
the cheerleaders
now fat and single
and brag about our children
then tell each other the truth
we called it venting
the good, the bad, the boring
our husbands' latest oddities
our children's teeny rebellions
we convinced each other
they were testing separation
and now she died.
The reverend speaks of her
and did not know her
he spouts on about life
after death, the glorious home
that awaits us all
and seems so certain
of what he doesn't know
and all that time
his hands moving
seemingly caressing
the very idea
of death.
What can one say of the dead but banalities?

The ride to grave is long through back streets
lights dim, all hushed, finally out of the city
and there the monuments to man's futility rise,
as once in a picture book she saw the pyramids.

V. The Shrine of the Dead

Angular shapes arch toward speckled sand
east of the languid fetid river
farmers scrape the soil praying for flood
that another rich harvest might fill them.
Round these thousand years the single plot
children beget men beget children
pushing themselves the wheel for water
and over all, Pharaoh and his tithe
the son of Ra, the son in his boat
crossing the heavens while bony men
cross their fields, a dull wood implement
to harvest corn.

From the East into the land of Khan
gradually came the tribes,
down to the muddy waters
to a land bereft of rain
a flat land crunched between sand.

Mene joined the two kingdoms, building Memphis.
He made a practical nation
ordering statues to serve dead lords
paintings to feed these corpses
studying heaven
irrigating soil
counting and writing
to gather taxes.
The God of earth, Keb,

long, thin, covered with stars
cut by the river
pinched by the desert
comprised the whole world
of serf, slave, artisan
noble and the Great House.
Zozar constructed his
terraced pyramid at Memphis
from the wealth of Egypt
and the conquered southern tribes
while Imphotep,
patron of scribes
god of healing
guided the nation
to prosper.
Author, architect, physician
administrator, he oversaw the copper mines,
contained Nubia
guided to prosperity
his building people.
Larger and larger tombs
they built, molding the land,
the flat, sand embraced
river bisected ground,
with stone mountains.
Khufu covered thirteen acres
a hundred thousand serfs
struggling to pile boulders
artisans of hunger and boredom
twenty years building.
The sons of Khufu
ordered the nation's wealth
to his grave.
And on the walls they wrote

I have entered into death
as a man of no understanding

and I shall come forth strong
and I shall look upon my form
which shall be that of men and women
forever and forever.
Then the priests of Ra
and governors of nomes
rose to greater power.
Pharaoh vied with them
his tomb shrunk
that theirs could be enlarged.
Above all locked in the desert, shine the pyramids
white as the sands clasping their base,
above all, save the sun born to die each night.
Ra riseth and seteth in the heavens of day
in his sectect boat he journeys across the sky
oh Ra, thou who art in me and I in thee.
The solid stone shines on the night of death
let me go thither as a mighty spirit.
Revolution by the southern tribes
dragged Mernere from his feast.
That mighty king regained the land
fertilized by the dead,
conquerors and conquered.
Thus Mazoi, Irthet and Wawat
bowed before Pharaoh.
Weaker kings reigned
while local monarchs
divided the nation.
Mentuhotep marched north
reuniting the kingdom
his children seized alien lands
gathered tribute to build Thebes.

I was father to the orphan
husband to the widow
shelter to the homeless
thus may I stand before Osiris

the forty-two judges looking on
to triumph over the tomb.
Sesustris' troops gathered gold from Kush
rouge from Absha pottery from the Hittites
mined Sinai.
The king is food
and his mouth increase.
The labor of the nation
built dams, temples,
brick tombs for king and noble
then the families of kings died.
Ruler followed ruler.
Hyksos came from the east
conquering the sapped nation.
The desert people
entered the land.
Filthy slaves, barbarians
fit only for rough finishing
and dragging stones
for the soaring monuments
it is rumored they pray
to an absurd deity
who, they say,
rules the world
but permits them to eat dust.
Their bodies stink,
desert rats
who defy Pharaoh
even in their rags
and if we are attacked
will these proud serfs
not join our enemies
so we will, it is told,
destroy this tumor
in our great nation
by working them
to be too tired

to plot against us
or build their little
rock piles for speaking
to their imaginary god.
Thutmouse spent his becoming years
a priest to Amon in Karnak
born of the king's mistress.
Then, rising to the crown,
he strengthened the kingdom
year after year inexorably
conquered east and south,
crossed the Euphrates,
ended tax-gatherers' corruption
gathered tribute from the world
led his armies in battle,
but alone in his temple,
guards, priests, concubines
in other rooms of his house,
he molded pottery
of translucent delicacy.

"I have risen
like the mighty hawk of gold
that cometh forth from his egg
I have risen---grant that I
soar like a bird to the presence of Ra,"
thus saith the mighty, then the lowly.
All will come forth through death
delivered from the four crocodiles
the serpent-fiend Seksek pass them by.

The heirs of Thutmose
hunted lions daintily
held festivals of ships and singing
and the Hittites nibbled the empire
gobbling it while Ikhnaton
secluded with his wife, daughters,

and priests in Akhetaton,
wrote hymns to his one god,
Aton, embodied in the sun,
his god of the world of Egypt
to whom fish leaped in praise.
Akhenaton imploring the one disc
Nefertiti, his dwarfed image
arms extended in haughty supplication
Man-god acknowledging solar deity.
A servitor aping his master's prayer
wishing Isis' and Osiris' forgiveness
for the necessary desecration.
The peasants crept from home
to bury their fathers
in little plots, scraped
at the base of the pyramid.

Harmhab chief of the army
proclaimed king by the oracle of Amon,
returned to Egypt its hoary gods
enriched their priests
punished the grafters
allied Egypt with the Hittites
too powerful to conquer.
Thronging to Pharaoh
thousands prayed for rich crops
feast and famine in one body.
They saw his golden house
envied him his servants
his great harem.
The High priest of Amon-Ra
in saffron and gold
stands at Horus' side
god with his flail and crook
crossed over his chest
looming motionless over them
while the savant, arms uplifted,

chants for fertility.
Then the proles
went back to plant
draw water and wait.
Seti marched on Canaan
recovering little of the ancient conquests.
Ramses II attacked the Hittites
a lion to the right of his chariot
fought at Kedesh, and marched back again
year after year returned to Syria
fifteen times until peace,
no land taken but graves.
Ramses growing old built new temples
pouring the remaining gold into them
hired soldiers to guard the frontiers
while the nobles gorged
on foodstuff of Cyprus
Babylonia and Naharin.
The people prayed to Baal, Astarte.
Libyans moved across the southern Delta.
Merneftah, Ramses' wizened son,
inherited the throne.
The cities of Asia revolted.
He marched into Canaan
subduing Askalon, Gezer and Israel,
forced back the Lybians
but the old ruled so long
there was no prince.
Kings rose in Nubia
to be slain at Thebes.
Each city became a nation
famine shrivelled the land
peasants homeless.
Then Seknakhat
took the double crown
slew the rebels
cleansed the throne of Egypt

and died.
From the north
barbarians moved through Syria,
engulfing the Hittite colonies
conquered by Ramses III,
their tribute Ramses
lavished on his gods.
Indolent priests gutted the people
peddling charms and incantations,
bought slaves
to farm their fertile fields,
tend their great flocks,
sail their many ships,
while the crown's laborers
starved building the temples.
Syrian slaves ruled the nation
from Pharaoh's household
Libya and Asia peopled the army,
the courtiers planned regicide,
discovered, were judged and killed.
Soon Pharaoh followed to Osiris' throne.
The Delta seceded
Syria and Palestine drifted away
the empire grew ragged
priests ruled the south
Lybians ruled the north,
the land chopped into little states
reunited under Piankhi of Nubia
a respite before the fall.
Roads, canals eroded.

Assyria moved west
conquered the delta, then south,
sacking the temples,
taking to Ninevah
that great city
those golden idols,

silver obelisks.
Then Persia under Cambyses
carted away the leavings.
Macedonia's son, Alexander
marched the great waste
stared at the rotting pyramids,
finally Rome took the land.

Let me eat the cakes of Osiris
on the eastern side of the Lake of Flowers.

Having lived a life which is good
let me cross the heavens in the boat of Ra.

VI. At the Grave

The tired second eulogy
ended, mourners leave
that brown pack of earth
with its tiny tag;
all gone but one, her friend,
who saw her ill just once,
withdrawing into the womb
of denial, and thinks
"From the reverend's words
what was she but daughter,
wife, mother and dead?"
And I, what more could he say?
university trained who now reads
Women's Home Companion, no books.
I bore two children
who others teach while I,
in reverie watch pictures,
play bridge and shop.
When young I learned of man,

the earth, of love,
thought of the universe and God

and where is God now?
a memory reincarnated
when the children are ill
and sometimes, rarely, in church.

Staring at the bare brown plot
How strange, the sun is shining
in striated yellow rays
striking a bush next to the grave
which seems aflame an instant
then dowsed and she is alone
staring at the bare brown plot
her mind drops back
to the beginning--the wondering,
drifting dunes, oasis, well.

VII. The Remnant

The first wanderer fled Ur
seeking substance of his void
hidden amidst commerce.
Out onto the sands he went
taking his household, flocks
to graze. Seeing the star,
the sun, the single moon
slowly God entered him.
Avrom, in trembling, called loud
his son of withered age
together they approached Moriah
to do the Lord's will. The slow ascent
heavy bearing the knife
wearily the father halted

to return but could not
nor could he climb. Finally,
feet dragged like roots from earth
he reached the top, built the alter
binding the sacrifice
blade poised, "CEASE"
thus compassion was given man.
Avrom begat Yitzhak begat Yakov
not in that order for the blessing
takes tortuous routes.

God needed these lonely men
to make Him known
and made extravagant promises,
the confirmation in blood.

The young chassid, earlocks long,
thin, pale from years of study
shuffles, skullcap pinned to his head,
the beginning of his dark beard peeping.
He wears a black frock coat.
"Dear Lord, why do You not provide?
I study Your law and go hungry
the worshipers of Mammon are bulbous
while I am a pile of spokes.
Is this how You reward Your faithful?
And Lord, if You will not make me fat
maybe a piece of meat a day,
or once a week at least."
Some little boys see the student
toss curses and rocks on him
as he runs toward the house of study
his threadbare coat flapping.

The night is dark, this night, this cold vast night
is cloud filled, fantastic shapes forming and reforming
high on the threshold of the world of God.

And Jacob, a nomad on life's pilgrimage
seeking a wife to fulfill his earthly course
rests, a rock his pillow, his cloak
a net between him and the cold
and the clouds, grey against the yellow stars
the moon, full, and him filled with the blessing
of deceit. The wind bites, blowing the cotton clouds
rushing against one another in passionate waltz.
And drowsy, weary with the flight from home
thought filled and thoughtless finally down, sleeps.

A ladder pale in the blue of his dream
stands and staring he can see no end
but strives to climb, his body sleeps.
Devoid of life as the stone beneath his head
he squints at forms, white shapes
wafting down through clouds then rising
arms outstretched he strains to touch
the tip of those billowing gowns--he fails.
THE VOICE--booming as an avalanche
"And thy seed shall be as the sands of the earth...."

He wakes and is afraid at the terrible prophecy
and builds an altar and prays and trembling goes
out into the lands of his wondering.

Spinosa sat in Antwerp
grinding lenses
splitting the Godhood
separated from kin.

They went into Egypt a tribe
peacefully grazing their flocks,
then the lash, for they were strange
and the mighty wished eternal homes.
Their seed was trampled
as dust, kneaded as clay.

Crying to God in misery
weeping for deliverance
finally no tears.
The Lord raised Moses
guided him to Pharaoh's house
sent frogs, boils, famine
slayed Egypt's children
and sent His people out.
They clustered at Sinai.
There Moses built an alter,
prayed beneath the mountain.
Thunder and lightning flashed
rain in the boom of heaven's voice
pounded the earth, the tribes
huddling in fear.
Finally the law was given Israel.
While studying, the slaves died
the men marched into the land
to build a holy nation.

Chanting in guttural monotone
five men squat in the temple
scratching chins beneath disheveled beards
reading Midrash, disputing interpretations.
the room is dark, no windows,
clogged in dust and pondering.
A man, learned of scientific truth said
when Joshua slew the Amorites
the earth must stop its turning
round the sun. But God
so made the earth
that on that day
the time was given.

The Lord had Gideon weed the army
of fearful, of dog-like,
and with his company

dispersed Midian
an hundred thousand slain.
The land returned to peace
and worshiped Baal-berith.

Then Tola, then Jair watched
and the children adored Baalim and Ashtaroth.

We have sinned, we have done abominations.

I cry to my God
for peace but there is war
for the dead, so many, I weep.

We are blameworthy.

Judah, whose flesh was peeled
ideals betrayed, rights of others denied
Ishmael beheaded
defamed, perverted righteousness
condemned falsely, presumed much
Akiba flailed
violent, slanderers, evil advisors
liars, scorners, rebellious against good
Hanina scalded wrapped in Torah
cursed, cheated, perverse,
denied God's word, oppressed
prideful, wicked--all
Simon, Chuzpit, Isebub
all slain for teaching the law
corrupted and corrupted
acting as swine
astray and leading others astray
God pardon, forgive, mold us.

David in his golden house
Solomon's seeds spinning

peered down at Bathsheba
the battlements of empire
the silken binding of the law
the moment before Goliath
escape from Saul
dead Jonathan
lyre and songs
Thou Shalt Not Kill
all forgotten
in that moment of lust.

Diana-Bathsheba
stretching nude in sunshine
under the king's gaze
her body open want
unfilled by old Uriah.
There where Abraham was spared Isaac
they built the temple of the Lord.

The rock trembling at my hand's caress
or do only the fingers pulsate
the American, helped don tefilin
for the first time since bar-mitzvah
Chassid's pais like camel tails
in innocence prostituting their prayers.
The great two-thousand-year stones
tiny cracks, bubbles, a ripple
a discoloration.
With the temperament
of a medieval monk I would choose
to live at the base of that rock
studying its crevices for the eye of God.

The people like leprous beasts
driven past flaking ruins to Babalonia
where the rabbis squat, teaching,
making the Talmud.

Then the first return.
Syria descended on the barren land
and the Maccabees from the hill country
freed Israel for a so short time
until the masters of the earth
returned, defiling the temple.
In rags they went to Spain
and brought forth Moses ben Maimon
and in the year Cristobal Columbus
went sailing to the spice islands
the house of Aragon decreed
the people shall be saved or dead,
the secret tearing of the wrack.
Some fled, died, apostatized,
kept faith in cellars
forgetting, finally, the scrolls
but loving the Father the King.
In Toledo, now, a hump backed
rib cage bumpety legged grey
ruin, somewhat hermaphroditic
descendant of sons of incest
a seller of oranges
joins his seventeen colleagues
all cousins to pray
four hundred year
remembered jumbled cacophony
still in a cellar's cellar
not believing their kin
went out and remade a land.

The Baal Shem danced, angels laughing
while God on high, seeing the disciples
rise and heels tapping, clapping, chanting
frenzied whirl of kaftan, pondered Messiah's time.

They bred prophets, Freud, Marx
while crying to return to Israel

escaped instead to America
where Cardozo and Brandeis
could judge and Javits legislate
and a haberdasher urge his old partner
recognize Hertzel's and Ben Gurian's handiwork.

God chose Dreyfus to ignite Hertzel, Weitzmann,
children shoved pennies in blue cans
to buy a plot and a tree
and from the pale, the boot, the earth's ghettos
came the pinched, kicked, rat-bitten
to tear at the land, plant, grow oranges
people the kibbutz with scythe and rifle
but some still squatted on Rothschild's dole.

The paper taken up with longing
"His Majesty's government view with favor
the establishment in Palestine
of a national home for the Jewish people."
So much white paper
forgotten when time to abandon rifles,
at Tel Hai, Trumpeldor led the settlers

most dead but the bricks endured.

Six million, an unknowable number
Anne Frank is real but six million skulls,
twelve million tibia, sixty million fingers
and how many teeth buried in known and unknown pits?

One man, charismatic
in screaming arrogance
impotent, with his clique
of moronic shrewd
black shirted bullies.
Sing rolladay and rolladay
the world watches the oft climbed bantam circle

of trucks to the west ride in long convoy
to the terrible blood gutted place of death
riding, bearing weapons many will frightened never use,
play follow the leader, sing rolladay.

Sing rolladay and rollanight
the stars shine magnanimously on the tank filled earth
at the tiny dots of shells blasting fiercely flesh
at the screams and bits of bone, the arm torn loose
the fellowship atones for some, but not for this,
play follow the leader, sing rolladay.

Sing rolladay and rollaway
the sun smiles on the last-night place of horror
now quiet but for the shrieks of some dying
now silent with the little patches of brown grass
turned black with coagulated blood
play follow the leader, sing rolladay.
In their glory daze they killed
long-distance and in a tiny
windowless basement bunker
left their little lives
and burned their bodies.

We are chosen
rudderless craft
no security of place
or time.
Auschwitz, Babi Yar, Buchenwald
guttural evocations of horrors
thought cannot adsorb
but droplets, as a single shoe
one lampshade, a soap bar
My God, what hath man wrought
upon man, we would not use
a flower so or soil a fly.
But there sat old bookkeeper Eichmann

plotting orderly shipments of goods
in pre-computer times and saying
pursed lips purged of repentance
he only did his duty.
Out of the ovens
the edge of ravines, the chambers,
skeletal eyeballs rolled up
like zombies unsensing
they came to Israel,
the vision past Dreyfus's scabs
to breed an oasis, to flower sand.

Spokes and flesh as shadow figures
they returned from the ovens,
Denmark via Sweden, Tripoli,
Arabia, the few of Treblinka
caressing the land in love's forgotten passion.
From spent and flagellated loins
heroes of Sharim El-Sheik
blitz of Suez
victors of the wailing wall.
Waterers, planters, reapers of the desert
able with skillet, gun and harvester
holders of the sacred land from those
wishing their annihilation.

At Warsaw bottles could not long
restrain the Wermacht tanks

but better to defend than troop to death
but better to survive like lowing oxen
to abet the ending two-thousand years patience,
Messiahless.
As Joshua blasting walls
with the roar of the shofar,
the forty years of Moses fifty times relived
manna withheld, water still rock bound

they bombed the squatting planes
hurtling from the north like rocks
flung from a sling and pivoting
raced east to bomb again.
Cyclops led, the tanks
sons of Ixion tread the desert
terrorizing their foes.
The kaftan bowed bandy backed beggar
Shylock pais framing palms grinding
stereotypes ground in the dance of war.

The forty four guardians of Sharm El Shiek
withdrawn, Haman decreed death to all the chosen
the planes gliding from the north hauling bombs
then east then west again--the tanks into Sinai
past Bethlehem, men dropped at the Straits of Tiran
in Jerusalem that holy mountain,
the first soldier
gained the temple wall, weeping, cold stones
of thousand years longing.
El Arish flanked,
Bir Gifgaga seized, the race to Mitta
and soon the canal, while diplomats
in New York spat curses and explanations.
And where in the end will it begin
and when swords made to plow
when will the lion and the lamb caress
who wean the returning king?

We returned to Israel
with tourists' cameras and flight bags
swooping down the Mediterranean
into Lod then past the great forests
Weitzmann, Truman, the slender
green-black cypress in bloom
the phallus of Van Gogh's madness
up the rock encrusted land

barren yesterday
now with the sabra also the orange
olive trees puffed against the sky
moving swiftly down the valleys,
past the headstones of rusting steel
finally the city of David
glimpsed through clouds and
two thousand years of weeping
like a new born rainbow
the city of stone Yerushaliem.
The wall, looming like a great mountain of God
the young men praying frantically beneath its boulders
each crack stuffed with new made prayers
oh the generations who only imagined it
the millions kept back by guns
the men who died to reach its great grey stones.

VIII. Mid Afternoon

She trudges toward her car
bent like the old woman she might be.
It's ages since I was young.
I remember visiting the museum,
that temple on the hill
next the river, columns
soaring against the cityscape,
wondrous paintings, sculpture,
the temple uprooted from India
Christ crucified, a sermon stronger
than any given by our minister,
the delicate tea house
and several times in college
I went to the gilded hall
to hear the orchestra
its strings soaring in harmony

there are no words for that sound
but my thighs pulsated
with the horns and drums
I haven't been back since then.
And so, leaving her friend
she drives the divided highway
the expressway along the river
shells, joggers barely glimpsed.
Past the indian, the father of the princess,
the garden of wedding pictures
her sight blurred with reverie
drives the ramp, diagonal parks,
pays her fee and walks the great stair
past tapestries through the hall
enters the room of saints,
madonnas, Christ crucified,
rushes from there in tears
to the room of urns, figures embracing,
dancing, copulating, she frowns.
Why am I so taken for granted
my husband appears for dinner
hunched over the soup course
like a bear lapping a lake
and awaits his steak and potatoes
a grunted thank you perhaps
at the meal's finis.
The children
arrive and disappear
not noticing me
except for their interminable
Mom, can I, will you, will dad
I need, I must have, I want.
Oh, but I love them
wondering how they feel
they will leave so soon
to college, work and wives.
Will their wives, as I did,

quit their jobs to raise them
and what will I do when
they have left?
What did I lose
those fifteen years
for so short a time
I was an editor of books
can I walk back in
reclaim my desk
laughing at my extended week-end.
Oh God, what will I do
I have felt at times
myself a solitary sponge
wife to him and them by rote.
I might have been editor and chief.
It was worth it, I think.
But what will I become?
Her stomach growls
she finds the hamburger restaurant
at the basement and eats
not tasting the tasteless meal.
Leaves the great building
with its Doric columns
leaves the busts, the urns
and drives to meet her husband
to drive him home before he
travels for business
as they had planned
last night before
falling asleep.

IX. The Dragon Slayers

Of water, the first principle
or all of air, but infinite

its nature out of dragons.
Embossed--the procession
round the march of Dionysus
chariots, immobile, calm
a centaur's death grapple
with mighty earthlings
pulsating forearms
blood gorged foreheads
interlacing flesh,
swelling of death.

Great in the hump of darkness
driving foreleg into this mud
huge nostrils, treetrunk horns
of the maze sunk in the black hill
green squares fired by the sun
grey clumps of rock
heaped piles of stone
flecked with yellow moss
waits the noxious presence.
Ikarus jerky rising to the sky
there hurled landward as a thunderbolt
but in that moment of flight
dazzled by intensity of light.
While Daedulus the artisan
aching of arm and loss of child
limps on across the sun's shadow.
The blind singer of Chios
gathering legends of his race
of simpering gods and patriarchs,
tribes herding atop craggy land.
Their mercenaries fought in Egypt
and stayed to deal in pottery
a peculiar people in the land of death.

Slender columned temple to the sun
all shimmering as the gowns of priestesses

of aged Pythia crumpled in trance
speaking tongues with eyes depressed
swaying suddenly, voice alto
divinely interpreted while subterra
sulphurous gasses hissed forth
of the rancid python
killed by Apollo.
Thus revealed the future,
thus the city states allied.

From tyrants, roasting their foes,
slicing nobles like stalks of wheat,
came Lycurgus raising Ephors
decreeing all obey the laws
and shave their moustaches.
Weakling infants were killed
children gathered into packs
of thoughtless warriors
seeking flagellation to honor Artemis.

White shirted slightly sweating
he, florid under Florida sun
watches twenty-two ox of men
beat at each other
to move a ball one hundred yards.
He grunts as the fullback
breaking a tackle goes nine more feet
first down--the center
with a dislocated shoulder
is lugged off on a litter.

At Marathon the Athenians
led by Miltrades, exile of Thrace,
waited while Persia, impatient,
divided its men. Then the sudden stroke
weak body and mighty pincers
the toll of slaughter, spear on bone

pierce veins and death
oozing into soil, blood, back
to the streams of earth.
But the hero, crimson in victory
sailed to seize Paros
and gangrenous, returned,
to trial and death.
thus to tyrants, at times.

Themistocles, poor
with no education of finery
built ships with silver profits.

Bules and Sperthias sent from Sparta
as scapegoats for Xerxes' heralds,
were spared and disappeared from memory.
Then Xerxes' army and fleet
mighty beyond ancient reckoning
entered Europe, crossed the Hellespont
through Thrace into Macedonia
down to Thermopolae where
the few withstood them until
by deceit they were surrounded
and died. At Salamis the great armada
destroyed. At Plataea the Persian army
decimated.
Athens rebuilt, the citizens
prideful of the burning and the victory
drove out the Persians and led the Delian League.
These Greeks eat the hand that saves them--
driving Themisticles into enemy service,
Pausanias, near death plotting with his foes
bricked into a shrine to shrivel
and dragged out to die. Cimon defeating
Persia at the Eurymedon on water and land
was ostracized by Athens, whose fleet
demolished in Egypt--Pericles' disaster,

and a truce at last with Persia and Callias.
Swiftly Pericles built a new empire
using his allies' taxes to craft the Parthenon.
Deep and silent in the molten core of earth
enveloped in terror of ferrous bubbles
the weight, oh God the weight
of all the buildings, smoke stacks
mountains, trees, shoes
horse-droppings, oceans, tad poles
pressing on my fetal body.
There visions of darkness
forever time continuing
but me at the world's intestine
thoughts, dreamings, progeny dead.
Memory of me receding
a name in an antique phone book
a rotting tombstone
a plaque in church
until building, rock and paper
all decay, then gone.

These little states, global dreams
of conquest like bathtub ducks,
one sinks and up pops one
one cracks, a new one's built.
Exercise the body to race, to kill
and dream outlandish rationalizations
paint those banners to lead the fools
to stab--ephemeral lives thus shortened.
Those noble disputations at the Parthenon
the plays given Dionysus,
the laws, the lovely balance
of mind and body
all dung before the hemlock cup.

Demeter, the mother, in Hades
seeking her child to bring forth

life upon the burnt earth
Artemis the fecund virgin
of harvest, maidens bearing
their locks as offering.

In prosperity, the arid earth yields
grain, olives, grape, figs,
the sea gives salt to barter for slaves
and fish, shark, eel,
honey and cheese to eat after pork.

She home, tending the children
docilely waits, cooking, spinning
while with golden hair and flowered gown
Diotema, accompanied by philosophical
chatterings, caresses his chest
languidly leads him to her couch
on which so many drachmas
have been spilled.
Phryne rising from the sea,
Aphrodite to Praxiteles,
slept with thousands
grew rich and finally old.

They sought learning
grasped the universe
in the sun crossing the moon,
in the core of matter
peering into man
sloughing myths
they explored all worlds
within their minds
all is one truth
said Parmenides
one being. Zeno
who proved arrows do not fly
was killed opposing

the tyrant Nearches.
Protagoras, agnostic
was flung from Athens
his books burned in the agora.

The husband of Xanthippe
fat paunched roamed barefoot
wearing his one robe.
Lover of the whore Theodota
and the boy Charmides.
Warrior in his youth
hero at Delium and Potiduea
satyr's face at martyr's end.
He quested wisdom
teaching to wish nothing
is to near the godhead.

Dressed in black suit
clutching his dispatch case
the husband-father
off the eight oh three
scowls at the artist
feet black, bearded
shirt in tatters
chinos paint spattered
hair long flecked in ocher.

Brazenly pacing Athens
Socrates taught the god of each man
rises above the law of gods or men.

There, high, an ant tied to the hot rock
torn by the vulture
agonized by the curse of life
the fire giver, shipwright,
philosopher, artisan
curses the gods

until, finally
the truce of resignation.
Boys, proposing ultimatums,
Corinth faced Athens at Corcyra
Athens attacked Potidaea
to preserve the empire
maintain the peace,
boycott preceded conditions
faces died to be saved.
At Sphacteria Athens victorious
was offered peace
but the rulers, safe,
from war's cannibalism
eschewed compromise
decreed a few more die
and finally settled at Nicias.
The fifty year peace
lasted six when
Alcibiades, nuevo power,
decreed more be maimed.

Ring-a-round the rosy
dance of bullets, severed arms
gored bellies, the principle,
whatever the hell it is,
for this year's cause
is next world's burlesque.
Remember the Maine, Alamo
war to END ALL WARS,
fifty four forty or die,
murder to stop killing.
Better send the old
supercilious senators
with rifles on their necks
bullets at their butts
and watch the peace come quick.

Lysander conquered Athens
after its generals
were executed.
The princelings returned
killing their enemies
censored speech
embezzled public funds.
Disgusted, the citizens exiled the thirty,
restoring democracy.
The law
sheaths, in words of ancient
rectitude the phobias
of the masses. Thus
man is martyred on the wrack
of righteousness--the indictment:
Socrates is a public menace
denying the gods of the nation
offending by corrupting its youth.
The defense:
What has been said,
now and of old is false, but never
shall I cease to speculate, to teach
I shall obey god, not man,
the state must be prodded to life
by those who do not accept
today's wisdom, who rail
against yesterday's truth.
So they killed him, the old man
of seventy and repented later
and built a statue to his memory.
The petty states clawed each other
Sparta, Thebes, Athens
felling all those beautiful young men.

The hump backed billy bandied beggar
beak awry, screams at the shaded sun
in the trash filled alley where driven

by the boys of blue, he picks papers
to sell to eat. Rag tattered he shuffles
like a bulbous question mark
between the ash cans and finds here
a gap tattered comb, here a shredded vest,
here a violin bow bereft of fiddle.
And skipping he hums delirious melodies.
In a valley in summer he sleeps
beside the gilded hay, smelling the dew
white and rising in rings from the sea-green grass.
The farmer hurls him from his contemplation,
dumb, bear-like he scurries to the city.

Demosthenes Jones is a humble man of the people
lawyer out of State College
trying for town council
with a party-packaged list of issues
a throat lozenge and disposable tissues
to pat the sweat from a visit
in August to the mill for votes.
A pocket notebook of quotes
for all polisticking questions
a file of voters in sections
by religion, income and point of view
most likely to please and tease
a vote from their narrowminded
cerebellums. The candidate,
dreams of national prominence
dancing like sugarplums
prays that he might represent
all of the people.

Squire Blood and Mrs. Hood
went strolling out one Sunday
quoth Squire Blood to Mrs. Hood
tomorrow is a quandary.

Dionysus of Syracuse, the old tyrant
scribbler of poesy, played the round
of war, victory and defeat.
When criticized by Plato
sold him as a slave
and ended drunk dead.

Phillip conquered Greece,
made ready to campaign east.
His time was spent
planning war, training his army,
plotting strategy, killing,
until Pausanias slew him,
bringing the boy, Alexander, to rule.
Diogenes, philosopher of the poor;
Aristippus, teacher of pleasure;
which shall we choose?
Oh man of thought and vanity
to feel all, through our few senses
for that short year given
or beg, drift across the land
owning nothing, sleeping in a vat?
But owning much, we can lose much,
fear tomorrow, but having nothing
never nibble the lust for power, drink
rich burgundy with crisp duck,
caress soft cloth and skin,
chance much on the pull of a card.
Devoid of goods, am I not free
to enjoy a single violet?

The classifier, anthropologist, solon,
biologist, physicist, anatomist,
philosopher, chemist, logician,
meteorologist, teacher of kings
scribe to the scribes to come
of future dark kingdoms---

Aristotle, caressing his mistress
the courtesan Herpyllis
in the hollow of night's longing
questing to seek the sun
upon the heaving breast,
all knowledge of life
upon the rising thigh,
all good in that cave
of life's beginning.

Alexander, first hun, grandchild of Achilles.
There the wild stallion rearing,
racing through fields, unnameable
until the great ride of giants
the boy breaking Bucephalus,
his father's shouts of pride
echoing on his spent body.
Fed on philosophers and soothsayers
he went, a boy, to conquer,
defeating the armies of the east
he proclaimed himself son of god
child of Zeus-Ammon, pharaoh.
He tore his enemies to death
pierced their flesh, dragged them
behind horses, murdered Cleitus,
in sottish violence, who had
saved the king's life at the Granicus.
Thus the lords of the earth
marching out to end war
to unite all nations
to spread philosophy, teach truth
bring light to the heathens
finally on a brocade and vomit soaked
couch of drunkenness, dead.

X. The Return

They come home and sighing, she
seeks her children, but they
have come and gone to friends
and all is well in the world
home cleaned, dinner bubbling
she walks upstairs, kicks her shoes
into a corner and lies down
takes a book but lets it drop
to watch the television quiz show.

This world fades so quickly away
immersed in the yellow glow
from another earth of manikins.

Age drops very fast
into the little days of our laughter.
The girls of summer, skirts high,
thighs firm and breasts
like Thanksgiving apples of earlier times,
laugh worrying over their dates
after Saturday primping
their hair the gem of the ocean.
Then the little lines
of worry over mortgages,
tiffs, the husband's roving thoughts.

We feel ashen in our calves
the bit of grey in the mirror
children chattering our silliness
and see the crater of our graves.

The days of sun and pink thoughts
are returned to the gloom
and memory tosses up the earth.

With each clot dropping on the casket
I lost a year of my life
which isn't much of a loss.
These days have dissolved
into few memories,
awkward sweaty in anticipation
on first date, first love, first child
the years of forty and college
weld together.
We married
in a blaze of rum
in April
when it forgot to rain
and how happy
were my parents
and he was resigned
and I terrified
for a person I knew
a few months
and not knew at all
to vow to love
until I die
and he was no worse
than the others
and proved a reasonable
father, probably faithful
sometimes funny,
I had expected more.
I must forget or remember in sleep
I must pray to God to comfort
the lamb I was and the ram I am
to bless the boredom and unrealized hopes
to consecrate the weeping and longing
to no purpose but pity of me
to forgive the curses and desires
to save from the uncertainty of death.
Our fodder hollowed be thy dame

mellowed be thy decision
do not tempt me with longings
do not show me the land
and leave me the tomb.

XI. The Cross Of Flesh

Plodding through the hot mud street
bearing the four pronged pillar of affliction
on his bone-thin shoulders,
past the blase strollers
who glance, shrug and pass on.
He is exhausted, caring nothing
of the bit of future
little of the bit of past.
Friends, followers, gone
the few words spoken
in the seconds of life
almost forgotten.

The fog from far off hills descends
blacking the sun--the earth is dry.

Slowly the march up hill- the dead shall rise
slowly the cross plunged in earth- the dead shall rise
slow the ascension of flesh- the dead shall rise
slowly nails pierce bone- lightning chars the sky.

The apostles crossed the Jordan to Pella
hailed the temple's destruction
as messiah's final coming
and roamed to spread the glad tidings
gathering pagans in cold immersion.

Paul of Tarsus, that wicked city,

spared by the God of Jonah,
taught the sin of each man
salvation in Christ's love.
Thus God died and was reborn
thus sup of his body and of his blood.

They killed him
them with martini manners
and tiny pink smiles
they locked him in their rooms
smoking through filter tips
and coughing daintily in cupped palms.
They killed him
him who raced with stallions
caught mares in mid-flight
to ram home the fecund blow;
him who stood on mountain tops
out-bellowing the wind
staring down on stars
leaping through folds of heaven;
him they penned in
stared at like some preened cat
smiled at because he was not them
but they could not take him all.

Constantine took the martyred band
to dominion, riches, presiding
over the council that proclaimed
the divinity of Christ.
So very tired, old in fear
exalted with salvation's promise
on the crowd's blood roaring
upon boar's tooth
and soul soaring heavenward
but (forgive my doubt) if false,
if Christ were myth,
impossible.

Caesar decreed my death
for some great purpose
this earth of bondage, strain
must be the portal of eternal beauty
slaves must be saved
and the mighty brought low.

Thus chained
before the jeering few
their eyes godward
bodies left in the Colosseum sand
intestines mashed with the dirt
and finally, to the caves
interred in climbing columns
pushing over the stinking empire
whose feet had strode
the land of the apostles.
Jerome loathed beauty
praised virginity and looked ascource
at the flowering cleavage
the pursed mouth of the gentle maid.
Entombed in his cell, he purged
his dreams, withering his pale body.
The night moonless
rising from bed, his mistress asleep
Augustine stretched, scratched his belly
and in the first blinking
after love's release
thought on Christ, praying relief
accepting chastity in very moment.
In the beginning was the idea of a world
then the word and the earth formed
the idea of earth, beatitude of soul
and the evil of Satin, choose oh man
you may be your shadow on the wall of heaven
or the lusting beast below.
She lay in tossing sleep

the image of white wings
covering, covering
and a swan's flight cloudward.

Crossing the Danube, crushing Belgrade,
Sardinia, Narssus, burning Thessaly
seizing slaves from Scythia
Attila marched to Constantinople
the Roman empire ransoming itself
with disinterred gold.
Even that mighty land
from the seven hills to Britain, the east,
conquering Athens and Sparta, Hannibal,
cringed before the hun.
Razing the towns of Gaul
beaten at Catalawnia
he regrouped and marched the boot
to Rome where Leo persuaded him back,
saving the stinking remains a moment
dying on his conjugal bed
choked in blood.
Gaiseric bagged Rome, sacking the riches
stolen from Solomon's temple.
And so the nation died
an anthill in a landslide.

The cats, curled in the shade
long but puffed, speck the stones
falling down brick, the Colosseum,
the seats of the emperor are gone
all but the stone high against
watered blue sky, in tatters,
a deserted quarry where once
men were whipped to kill
for jaded rulers of man.
The cats climb along the brick
fortifications, built on the motes of blood,

the huddled, crying to Jesus.
Once Caesar strode and died
this city, king of the pantheon world
tugged strings and Gaul and Britain danced.
Then each pope in power or in guile
played Nero's tune and nations burned.
Once virgins tended these shrines
now marble chips like headstones
mark the temples, churches
with peeling facades
strung along Ionian columns
and there, embedded in the earth of Rome
the cats peer at gawking pilgrims
awaiting offerings of liver and brains.
Cheeks flecked of red
skin greying, cramped
of agony, dead
the rats murmur
a house, once heaped of marble
empty, left to the unseen scourge
like mosquitos in a sprayed bog
the bodies moldering, unmourned.

Fifty three times he led his armies
to the edge of the realm
Charlemagne, in one day
beheaded four thousand five hundred Saxons
and left to celebrate
the birth of Christ.
His juries deliberated
his counts ruled justly
and Istria, the extorter
was made to return his gains.
The rich were taxed
that the poor could eat,
schools built.
He was crowned great king

by papal fiat, to rule as divine
over the squabbling France fiefdoms.
Demiliterate, he built
a gentle bureaucracy
affected the costume of power
when needed
and the mask of rudeness
to rule.
Robert the Pius
shunned war, and with flattery
gifts and persuasion gained the earth.

The mighty knights of ages gone
off to save their women
from foul breathed monsters
in shining rectitude
all five feet of armoured
horses slavering at the battle
and gerkins lice infested
diddled the ladies in waiting
while waiting for glory.
Dragons were real men in those days.

At the moment before sleep
that great vibrant woman
who so pulled him into life
tore Benedict's thighs.
He plunged upon thorns
impaling his flesh as he had hers.
To her memory he created a life
for those to follow
silence, chastity, courtesy,
work, prayer, moderation,
self-flagellation.
Leo traveled the Christian world
seeking sinners, banning
the peddling of bishoprics,

damning the corrupt,
ordering confession
from his ministers.
In his age he led
his pitiful army
into Norman death
and at his last moment
squatting before his coffin
wept for the lives he cost.

Hildebrand, misshapen
advisor to lords
risen Pope as Gregory
sharp and ugly as a vise
screamed, conquer the Holy Land,
proclaiming celibacy of priests.
The master counselor of politicos
as Pope, moved against
the king of the Germans
courting war, losing Rome
gaining the hatred of millions
dying exiled unrepentant.

That vast company of tents at Clermont
lords greatly tutored in sin
seeking absolution and grandeur.
Urban stirred them with words
"we must conquer the aliens,
thou, God's chosen,
must defeat the barbarians
torturers of our kin
their land awaits you
which was our land
a land of milk and honey
greatness and divinity
shall be yours."

with the cross on their chests
and killing on their minds
they abandoned family
to conquer the Saracens
to do God's will.

The Maid
Air drifting in mad rushes
over soft fields, the mud deep
in the church road
Domremy by the Meuse.
A shrill toe of fire
piled at that tiny body
flesh pierced only by a barb
she opined the siege of Orleans
blessed as the Virgin, cursed as the devil,
taken at Compiegne, called heretic
she was sold to Warwick
and at the market of Rouen
with a blessed crucifix
she burned like a green branch.
What quantum of lives will we accept
to purge the deep-set lust
blanketing all in fire
yellow-red-green the flames
sulfur stenched, how many
bones shall lie in mold
crusted trenches, teeth rotting
before their fated end
to atone for maudlin phantasies
where will we cease,
what martyr the last?

Ferdinand and Isabella appointed a board
to sniff out heretics, bind Spain,
there was a bit of profit
from the cash of the condemned

to split with the well meaning informer.
Converted, then unconverted Jews
made good test cases.
The accused
won freedom by condemning kin.
The prisoner, in chains, no visitors
no counsel, presumed guilty
torture edged him toward confession,
and then, if he survived
an advocate could plead
over the broken bones.
Defense witnesses, whipped,
to prove their testimony truthful.
Hung by the wrists, drowned,
flesh cut, tendons mascicated,
bones snapped on the wrack.
And if convicted, the lash, slavery, death
by fire at the stake.
Efficient Torquemade worked fanatically
to secure all for heaven.
Contarini, the last hope of reconciliation,
drew Lutherans and Catholics together
on man's relationship to man
but failed with the Eucharist
and thus the crack of reform
became a chasm of hatred.

Paul declared war, anew,
on the children of the devil
burned the wisdom of the Hebrews
ordered censorship
excommunicated publishers
reactivated the Inquisition
its rules: speed, severity, intolerance.
Again neighbor spied on neighbor,
Cardinals denounced as heretics.
Friends of heretics, suspected heretics,

were traced and chained.
Unshakable in his faith, the pope
would burn his own father, he said,
and on Paul's death, the mob
burned his headquarters
freed his prisoners
and torched the inquisition's records.
In heaven, did God meet him
and thrust him down shouting
"THOU SHALT NOT KILL."
The world glistened, Lorenzo fought
and wrote to his unattainable love.
At twenty he ruled and knew
the fear the old enjoy of youth
convened a council of statesmen
to ratify his better judgment.
He led the balia in prosperity
from sculptured gardens,
managed the papacy's riches.
When Volteria expropriated his mine
he crushed the town.
Assassins, failing in their try
were hurled out windows
to cries of "long live the balls."
That night plotters and suspects
were hanged, stabbed, torn, drowned
by the gentle folk of Florence.
Naples warred on Lorenzo
the citizens, now wealthy,
muttered at the new taxes.
Il Magnifico sailed down
to death and returned in peace.
Athlete, poet, wit, adulterer,
philanthropist, philosopher,
scholar, farmer, embezzler,
employer of spies and predatory practice
dispenser of bread and circuses

sponsor, tyrant, bawd
the great prince, begetting popes, lionized
by Machiavelli, heaped up riches.
The effortless touch of palm on breast
soft caress down thigh
entrance into sticky core,
oh Lord, not yet chastity
not yet, and when memory
overcame desire
he took the Bishopric of Hippo
strong-willed, wise leader of men
he spread the gospel as he found it.
They flocked to be led
in conversion, asceticism,
as congregants.
His mind
wrestled the anomalies
free will, sin, evil, lust
interpreting the text as symbol
authoring his life and dreaming
his early joy and shame.
The heavenly home and earthly town
he showed assuaging the world's doubts
and died, as warrior, rallying his people
amid barbarian siege.

The good and gentle compromiser
in an age of extremity, is doomed,
ricocheting from high to low,
left to right, calmly reasoning
the hurricane to confine itself
to its eye, Erasmus
escaped to a monastery
begging the Pope and Luther
to sit and reason together.

Will, piping on cloven feet

singing of kings and twins
incest, fratricide, assassination
and all that down home humor
the witches stir eternally
his signature, on a deed in London,
the labored letters of an illiterate
but then Bacon wrote all that
or was it Anne Hathaway?

Failed minister, richly indulged
depressed by the death of Edward King
touring Rome with pomp and servants
and yet that pampered fop
wrote of joy, of sorrow
as a child playing.
Then he taught,
disputed on religion
married a child-dolt
deserted after one month,
and then returned to grant him
a lifetime of shrewishness.
He turned to politics
pled for freedom of speech
but suppressed royalist tractates
served as Cromwell's apologist
and went blind.
Two wives and his newborn infant
died, Parliament denounced him,
arrested, imprisoned, censored,
released and then he wrote
and finished amid the plague
Paradise Lost, sold for eighteen pounds.

Asleep, the terrible dream of flying,
shattering fall.
In delicate strokes
the lovely green framed lady

down that corridor
and over one room
from winged victory.
Designer of machines, unbuildable,
dissector of humanity
DaVinci, the owl.
Bastard, raised in luxury,
imprisoned for sodomy
twisted as a rope played by a cat
his release in paint and marble
and design of war material.
Writer, musician, architect, horseman,
mathematician, designer, inventor,
astronomer, cartographer, physicist,
anatomist, botanist
the list of his ists is the numerist.
He turned to the church to die.

Copernicus, son of a metal merchant
ward of a bishop, his uncle,
apprenticed to the Church, a cannon,
the sun and planets obsessed him.
He studied law, practiced medicine
taught mathematics at Rome
reformed Prussia's currency
but the stars blinded his thoughts.
Slowly, at Heilsberg, calculating
the movements of heaven and earth
the earth, a restless corner
of the universe, all this,
disseminated without trumpet blast
while he continued his calm life
condemned by Luther, criticized by Calvin.
Until wrenched by the boy Rheticas
into publication, and at that moment,
in the best of time, died.
The First Book of Revolutions

banned by the inquisition
but he was past the lash.

To build his church the pope,
son of Lorenzo
sent peddlers of virginity
lightly springing the wealthy
from purgatory.
How lovely to buy
at the corner shop
anticipatory absolution
three for a dollar, only
one venal sin per customer.
The monk denied that cash could buy
what love would not effect.
Tacking his thoughts to the castle-church door
to be pondered with the nineteen thousand saintly relics
the monk of Wittenberg, that petty town,
taught philosophy, God haunted
Jehovah the scowling,
he went to Rome
fresh from fasting and prayer
encountering wares, whores, wine and wealth.
Salvation is faith, not jewels.
At Augsburg, Cojetan and Luther met
one great in knowledge, one in rectitude,
that child of Satan was called to Rome,
refused and howled against the anti-Christ
sitting on the throne of Peter.
At Worms he faced the lords of earth
and bowed to no man but God
retreating to a cell at Wartburg.
While men railed against the Church
Luther counseled moderation
dressed in knight's clothing
like a wall, cracking at the top
and shattering at the foundation stones

the poor of the towns rose in armor
while poor old Luther whispered pro nobility
offering prayer and the hair shirt to the rebels.
He ate and drank vigorously
with his wife, children and foundlings,
denounced the papacy but prayed
the gospel not be defended by murder
and in his olden years
he proposed the death of heretics,
authority, an anchor of faith.
In great pounding phrases, when old,
he stung with the whip of the patriarchs
extolling his good, denouncing unbelievers,
and in his dotage and illness he proclaimed
God, through His rulers, breaks men
on the wrack, flogs flesh, makes war.

The hare is a gentle creature
it does not war as ants and man
it does not leap to the jugular from heights
as the tiger and man, it does not torture
as the cat and man
it does not imprison in immobile horror
as the honey pot ant and man,
it does not kill as the piranha
and as man.
Americus Columba nee Erickson
paddled the globular oceansee
for guild edged treasure
thirsting of beri buried booty
to hunt and kill the peaceful
Brahmins decedents of Noah
Shem, Ham, Jaapheth and their gods
Baal-Mammon-Istarte which they carted
on every prow and in their breasts.
This, the glorious land of promise
of mountain, canyon, red sunset

loam fields and miles of bison
by treaty, gift, gun, rum
seized from the tenants thereof
in perpetuity and evermore.
But first we must recall
the brave explorers of itching feet
and palms.
Henry the Navigator
governor of Ceuto, trapper
of blackamoors who, solemnly
baptized, were made to work the fields
of the noble Order of Jesus Christ.
And finally, after voyages in terror
DaGama reached India of spices
and jewels. Cort-Real, Cabral,
Amerigo Vespucci found the new land
their little boats swamped
again and then, sick but driven
by pride and greed, mastered storms
rotting wood, their skins baking black.
The Genoese weaver, Columbus
maker of maps, dreaming the wealth
of China. A fanatic, he negotiated
with Spain, France, England for ships
and finally, Santander shamed Isabella,
with dreams of converting nations,
to give Chris his Nina, Pinta and Saint Mary.
In calm weather, but lost in water
the crew pled then mutineered to return.

My life I have charted this course
plotted, platted awake and
dreamed it awake and asleep.
I have schemed, used friends,
lied---for this, days of water.
Fools for crewmen, hunger,
doubts, shall we sail on

and on and on until we die.
Have I misjudged, miscalculated
from optimism, hope or wanting.
They will think I dreamed of wealth
the spice and gold of the Khan.
Idiots! The queen may have it all.
I, son of a weaver, a kind man
who never thought beyond his city,
am doing what no one else dared.
Wealth! Silly trinkets! Who sails
the ends of the earth for silver?
My crew, fools who weep
at the first stomach cramp.
Why then? God knows!
Fame? What value that I,
dead, be remembered?
I must seek what none have seen
even to drive slave and king
to my will--I shall succeed
but if not--I have begun.
But "LAND." With beads and caps
he bought the love and possessions
of the inhabitants thereof.

Captain Cook dared sail the earth
killed by that wickedest, evilest
smelly one-armed villain, Hook
who found the fountain deLeon missed.
They bang off the planet
touch the moon in absurd getups

fat rectangles in white
hooked to earth through tubes
grubbing for rocks.
But soon they will come, as Lewis and Clark
to map, Jason, to seek the fleece
and new John Aldens and Adams

to found that calm and silent land.

Punch oh Punch. What is it my pet
I have something for you
what my sweet
come see yes Judy what is it
a bopsicleBoh I love popsicles
Here!

They emptied the prisons and dumped the indigent
on the Colonies, religious fanatics, dissidents
petitioners, second sons of proud families
they came, some in hope, most in desperation
chained together from Chad, in rags
from the shtetels, from the arid soil of Ireland,
Puerto Rico, Sicily---filling the East
and struggling West to the beat of Benet
and Greeley.
Blinking at the sudden light
paupers from the gaols of Merrie England
saw the misty street all shining
to escape the cell of doubt
they had failed or been failed
and now sail to the land of savages.
O'er the oseen the Smiths
and Minuets and all of
the Janet come latelies of the
DAR and Elks, MOOse
(but not a rabbit in the pack)
the descendants of the tract thieves
of your, arrived like locusts
roasted a few turkeys
before taking the continent.

Revere, the brassmaker
warned the citizens.
Dead in the riots, Attucks,

first martyr of the revolution
a raggedtagged bunch of long hair crazies
wanting to slice the cord to the
rotting civilization ruled by a paranoid.
The gentle hills of Valley Forge were refuge
to the hungry rebels, in mud-log huts
they marched to the Frenchman's beat
learning war from the Pole
while George, up at the big house
waited out the winter.
But him
sybarite that he was and jolly Ben,
civic do-gooder, tinkerer, spewer
of platitudes, whore-monger, rich
lusty old Ben, cajoled the pants
and bankrolls off the Parisians,
danced his way into the panties of a nation.
That's the way the confederation grew
from sea to shining see.
Her jewel box stands seven feet tall
with deep azure enamel inlay
golden hardware, flutings and pastels
Marie Antoinette, coiffed lisping
darling of dandies, fawnlings on the king
who could not bear solitude.
Builders of monuments, their court
away from the throng of dirty subjects.
The stretch of hedges, lawns fit only
for dainty feet, the great hall
lined with mirrors for the infinite
adoration of self.
They came, the rabble, breaking windows, like bison
grinding flowers to mud, shouting slogans
freedom-liberty-equality--except for the perfumed
cockatoos whose necks they sliced.
Then, like chickens mad to peck the blood spot
it turned upon itself, beheading Danton.

Blood gurgling from the mud
beneath the glimmering block.
Tapped once on his hard-to-turn back
old Marat knifed at bath,
Trotsky dead in Mexico. Boleyn beheaded.
In Salem senile crones were burned
for want of circuses and fairs.
In Spain the wrack for fun and profit
while Malcolm X and King and Bobby
lie moldering marching with John Brown's body.

Victims of man arise
throw off your shrouds
and blacken the sky in
vast multitudinous
wailing---all to no end,
your killers are mostly dead.
Divine right of kings we know
was not divine, nor right
we cheered the little colonel
Adolph Benedito Francisco
Duvalier Patrice Benedito
threw roses at his soles
sig heiled and viva'd him like god
his fantasies the wants of all
and so we all marched proudly
to Moscow dying by the bushkillfall
for the death of tyranny
the death of all.

When we were little boys
we hid and sought in words
don't tread on me, forty four forty
and abstruse doctrines
but there were Indians to bully
and that was good, for they were barbarian
needing a bit of old time religion

for the land they would not farm.
The French in 1812 were busy elsewhere
and not too hard to take, and Spain
far from its ports, sans armada
and the bones piled up
savages stuck on sandy waste
lands cleared of aliens
and a few nice islands
for rest and recreation.
Alaska was a coup
gotten over no one's body
we are bigger boys
and righteous--god's beloved.

His blood flicked the ceiling
at that mad instant
depression just past stasis
cypress like an asp's tongue
tips the sky and plunged
the moment of consciousness
after the razor slashed ear
yellow and red vases
fields of coagulating sunlight
green stucco off his palate knife.
There in the house of madness
raping pliant canvas
roaring into death.

Alexander was a boy
when he marched the farthest
tips of the earth.
Napoleon the conqueror
granted law to his civilized world
and China, that sophisticated empire,
remained at peace.
The glory of Hannibal and Caesar
was not in victory but dominion

orders obeyed shield the agony
that to a man, death follows kisses
in an unadorned tent
more glorious than mosaics.

Franco and Papa Doc danced a stately quadrille
most marvelous liberators of their people's purse
and slowly sashayed around the palace guard
and gently waltzed above the hungry masses
daintily frugged while women, in endless lines
silent, eyes sunk beyond weeping,
waited outside the marble prisons
to see their covertly taken husbands
for crimes of thought or thoughtlessness
unbailable, tried or untried
while Doc and Frank sensually tango.
One man, the fire maker
us warmed us
we shunned him, we laughed
because he would not hunt
and when he died, we built
a little tower to his memory.

The rock is dust
Atilla's name will never die.

Vladimir Zworkin, where are his pyramids?
our eyes are worn day and night
with his invention, the world turns,
doctors heal, lawyers defend
and suffering comes to life.
The arch of Hadrian
will ever stand.
Faraday we remember, for what?
and Einstein, but who has read his theories?
Robert Bakewell, Booker Washington.
David and Goliath, inseparable.

At Palmyra, New York
the angel of God came down
revealing the gold tablets
the glasses of translation.
Thus the Book.
This strange people of saints
naturally persecuted by neighbors
sought refuge in Ohio
then Missouri then at Nauvoo
in Illinois.
The people grew
and multiplied, converts
came from America and England
and Smith, the prophet and his
twenty seven wives lived in peace
until his martyrdom
in that awful stabbing.
His follower Young was allowed
to reach the promised land.

Laying cable in the North Sea
renting cars, building homes,
servicing the weary traveler
ruling communication
Geneen, the street emperor
of a mighty nation in nations,
corrupting the weak, creating wealth
his domain, manipulation of men
carefully drawn budgets
shining machinery.

Dreams of justice and sanity
what mad ideals of impractical men
Freud analyzed himself
and found all men
while Marx, analyzing all

discovered his own reflection.
Each one living content
satisfied in himself
and at his workbench.
To each his needs,
cash and ego.
But exploiters must die,
their exploiters, not ours.
Man is not an automobile
to run and trade in.
One man's death entombs me
his illness trembles me
Merry Christmas to all
and to all a good life.
Who was that lady
I saw you with
last night? That was
no lady, that was my id,
the entire cast of the Bolshoi
and the sixteenth Red Army.
Why did the robber baron cross the road?
to exploit the next field.
Three thousand inmates
of community psychiatric hospitals
drink a simultaneous toast
in gaitorade and gin.

From trench to tank corps
mustard gas to atomic bomb
big bertha to B-29
the ways of death are clever
just a bit of pruning
in the overpopulated forest
in such a good cause.
At Bataan hundreds were marched
in tatters, no food, feet bled to bone
until men became skeletons and dead.

Tales told in the headlines,
but my high school friend
never saw his father,
instead, a personally signed letter
from Franklin Roosevelt
told of the colonel's great bravery
and offered him admission
to Annapolis. He went later.
When the dough boys marched through Paris
there were cheers, the wine flowed
and God were we proud
the heroes of the war to end war
but mice climbed through
the barbed wire, chewing our rations
cannon shot pocked the viscous mud
occasionally tossing a leg cross field
and we cried Mamma in the night.
When it ended we rode Broadway
pelted with ticker tape
but it didn't seem so fine as Paris.
And then we went to Spain
as a lark, to show ourselves
we were men. It was a funny little war
with thousands of funny little men
dead.
We learned how to fight for real
with pincers and flanking movements
to isolate divisions, cut supply lines
with saturation bombing for cover
and tanks moving past static infantry
to kill en masse without seeing the dead.

The butcher of Buchenwald had God's power
who shall live and who shall die,
how live, how die, when,
the book always open
and he was gentle with his children.

When he kissed them
he left no blood on their lips.
There are various eyes of war
the eyes of the marine hoisting the flag,
atop Surabacci [not in the photo,
when he did it really].
The eyes of the Nazis marching the Champs
cold of revenge for the Versailles Treaty,
the million mark postage stamps.
The eyes of the machinist at Hiroshima
instantly blind and gasping *après moi* the bomb.
Delegates blinking wisely, tut-tutting
at goosestepping blackshirts
their crystal nights
and their maniac leader
while the grey senatorial nay
sayers, billions for defense
but no bucks for peace.

Scholar, drunkard, monkey man
each, in his own time displayed
to examination and cross examination
each, in his own place, opened
by the scalpel of truth searching
all guilty, Oppenheimer, McCarthy
and the obscure teacher Scopes.
Each a cause celebre
in his time and place
and each....what was the cause?
Check it in the footnotes
of the compendiums of history.
Roosevelt, feeble at death's end,
legs withered, memory failing.
Stalin, erect and insane
dreaming the kaleidoscope of empire.
Churchill, wise, articulate, impotent
destined to live in the midden of memory

smugly sat for their portrait
at Yalta after whacking up the real estate.
Power, held too long is belief
in one's omnipotence.
Then they hung Il Duce from a lamp post
and Hitler burned while Hess fiddled
fuhrerly dreams of owning the world
compressed within one dank bunker.
Power, held too long is delusion.
Power, held too long engenders madness.
Peer deep in this polluted lake
down black silted bottom
rusted cans, detergent foam
there is no reflection.

You, my neighbors
the late little boy
on tricycle, then
playing touch football
in the town park
oh, how you can kill.
And you, my aging countrymen
how in all of hell and here
can you imagine we should not speak of this
for fear of our effect on other nations.

Thou SHALT remember those
"males and females of various ages
whose names are unknown."
We can, of course, weep for the children
but they are simply dead.
Their elders knew their children's fate
before the bullet scream
and they could not escape
and knew not the nice little towns
that reared the booted trespassers.
Thou shalt not accept that men

have preyed on man these centuries.
Tales from the Crusades to Buchenwald
to Guernica to Songmy have been
of man the cannibal. The dust of our earth
hides bones of all those victims
whose victors live until they too
in time are scourged.
And that village of five hundred or so unknown names
attached to bodies that can no longer farm,
love and die surrounded by their grieving
on matted beds.
The fish lie bellies up, bloated hulks
upon the lake in which we peer
and cannot see ourselves.
The dead surpass grief,
I weep for me
for what I have wrought
beside the lake through time,
and last I weep for me and for
the whitening bones of Songmy.

XII. DAYS END

The house is quiet
the maid, cleaning the cellar
soap squish and bucket rattle
through the solid maple doors
is gone to her home.
She plods upstairs
wishing the children home
to shout hellos
kicks off her shoes
puts on slippers
picks a book from a case
of burnished mahogany
thick leather bound
bought as decoration
dusty, pages uncut
flips through slowly
glancing at words occasionally
but cannot read a sentence.
Why, oh God why did she die
under the dirt
the dank coffin.
She drops the book
turns on the T.V.
the quizmaster
oozes questions at the smiling
so slightly flushed
so very young
embarrassed greedy newlyweds
enshamentranced by their revelations
of first kiss, first gropings
the dress she wore
their honeymoon morning.
One couple merely went
to her parent's house.

And she, on her couch
had gone and found the apartment
and he adored it, so cozy
one room, but they loved
and in time found furniture
together, and in the cold
they held together for warmth
the great dreams--some happened--
but this house is now so very warm
and death is nearer and she is
faithful but why, why not?

Towers of brick and glass tumbling
unpainted to scrap littered pavement
smell of pizza, orange sweet syrup
mustard pungent piled on franks.
He, in day's end sweated jacket
and wrinkled white shirted
faces a little Mennonite in lace cap
a girl with frizzled hair, moustached
deliberately punching passers-by
singing loudly off key frenetically.
A socialist handbill spins
like a dust devil down the gutter
the electronic booming crash
rock music out the record store walls.

The wasted nun
eyes downcast
unseeing
gently molded face
slat arms
tapering fingers
offers her cup
silent.

Out past the black teen with homemade
shoeshine box. "Hey shine mister
Hey mister"
hearing a coin clink
in the nun's cup.
The squat woman
with hairy legs stands at her everyday place
her blind eyes beseeching the judge
who daily contributes his quarter
and strolls to the medieval turreted
gargoyled City Hall to face the accused.

The river front freighter disgorging
bananas, autos, oil, sailing upriver
with ore to the great foundry.
There, at the hot dog stand
Jefferson finished the Declaration,
Franklin, nearby, lugged his loaves,
and he, soot flecked, toward the train
this boring work day over, toiling
for her, and for the children
if only they lived simple again
but she needed the big house,
the maid, the big car. He
senses the city, drops a dime
into the nun's cup and into
the paper littered station for his train
finally toward the 6:15 for tree shaded
winding roaded suburban street
pushed toward his car, his stained seat
old springs pushing up his butt
reading the everyday same paper
feet touching tan dispatch case
all sitting purse lipped silent
thinking of cocktails and golf
with her at the club pool relaxed
moving past those standing in the aisle

down the steps and out the paint peeling
station to his rusted second car
waiting since morning at the lot
to home and wife, children, dinner.

He in undershirt and slippers
she in red flowered robe
one child asleep
the other at a friend's
they glance languidly
at that face
on the little screen
firm, healthy, each morning
he jogs, then breakfast
then tennis before the sessions
with wardrobe man, makeup man,
producer, director, business meeting
on how the campaign is to go
then finally paraded out
before the hades hot klieg lights
"Fellow penitents in God
as I look around this marvelous hall"
Oh Christ, he yells, must we
look at this soul saver one more moment?
Just one second, she answers
I want to hear him for just a minute.
"As I look around this great hall
I see the breath of Mammon
seekers after the possessions
of this world not after
the safety of your immortal
souls.
Come to me, join God's
blessed covenant."
Good God
let's go up to bed, he shouts
and she ascends.

XIII. EPILOGUE

In this night of longing, I, awake, and he
in bed asleep to the dim glow and muted
whisper of the television. Insomniac
sated with memory of the little me laughing
at my mother's cheek while she, humming
roasting a fat duck, awaiting my papa
in the crowded, cinnamon odored kitchen.
Then life was so easy, she cooked
washed, sang and diapered baby
and papa worked late, never grumbled,
there was no time. But he always said
I would go to college and make something
out of my life. And I did, and I didn't.
Papa died with unfulfilled wishes
and I live in unrealized potential.
My mind is filled with dreams, memory
I created life, and that was wonderful
they will be my fulfillment, I dream
doing day to day things only, dream
of birth and dying, me as martyr,
me as vestal virgin, me as priestess.
I would sacrifice my life to do wonders
but the deeds I imagine are being done.
I couldn't heal the sick, run for office,
teach the gospel, paint a masterpiece.
He tosses, pulling covers off my knee.
The air is cold, I search for comfort,
a cricket lusting off beyond the spruce
is happier in a life measured in minutes.

When I was a child, lacking wisdom,
I prayed with fingers clenched white
to become a queen bee, fertile,
fed, no questions asked. No papa

nor mama to comfort, but only me
at the core of the hive, growing fatter
in the wild fire--but peace I never knew.
What purpose am I, mother of two.
Tomorrow I'll wake to the clock radio
while he will hunch in his easy chair
watching Notre Dame-Purdue
shoving each over about a football
today's graveyard, the ground
so muddy, so damp
and each day sleepwalking
I must read Tolstoy
maybe back to school
I must, but now
tired, sleep
comes so long, his snores
comfort me, we talk
at times, and hug
and fight sometimes
but mostly in silence.
My mind sees yellow dots
white flashes riding
down the ramrod streets.
Why do I pray
why do I stay.
Like sleek brown foxes
terrified of horn and bark
why kill the strong
and cauterize the dying
let me sleep.
What world we've made
dementia become the norm
paranoia its thesis
flesh its antithesis
give me rest.
My children's lives
I hope for in good

they do not know me
my husband knows me not.
My god- no one, not even me.
I am mad of this earth
I would not do a flea
as man attends to man.
My stomach broils
I am deadened
as from an epidural
I cannot sleep
Holocaust reiterates
Bosnia, Chechnia, Iraq
SudanBthe names, rulers
should rot in hell
my children must not
inherit the world I've lived
grant me rest.

For my sins grant absolution
hail Mary, shema Israel
Jesus, Buddha, Zoroaster,
Gilgamish, Ra, Zeus,
Allah, Jehovah, Baal
give me peace
grant it my children
all children, my husband
my new dead friend,
save us all
PLEASE let me rest.
And finally sleep embraced
curled as at the moment
before her birth
the first cell
dividing in her breast
the first instant of her death.

Biography

Mitchell A. Kramer was born and lives in Philadelphia, Pennsylvania. He graduated from Dartmouth College and Yale Law School. *Valley of the Shadows*, his first book of poetry, was published while he was in law school. He began writing *Her Couch of Silence*, his epic poem, as a young lawyer and completed it forty years later. He has practiced law in Philadelphia for over 50 years after having served as a Deputy Attorney General of Pennsylvania.

Poetry writing is his passion. Every weekend he can be found on his porch with his trademark cigar and his pen and notebook. These poems are a small selection of his writings.